Creative Expectancy

Creative Expectancy

. . .

Albert McClellan

BROADMAN PRESS
Nashville, Tennessee

Library of Congress Catalog Card Number: 78–128856
Dewey Decimal Classification: 248.4
Printed in the United States of America
20.N70KSP

Contents

CHAPTER 1

The Challenge to Creativity

. . .

A popular song relates an event in the life of a little girl and asks in refrain, "Is that all?" The song then describes one by one other life events and repeats: "Is that all?" This is the unanswered question in the lives of most of us. We want to know, Have we had it? Or is there more to come? We have a great hunger to be something more than we are.

This drive to find freshness and variety in life is the creative impulse of man and one of the signs that he was made in the image of God. It is the impulse of following in God's footsteps, taking nothing and making something out of it. God has given us this creative impulse to help us find our own special answer to the question, Is this all there is to life? He means for us to seize the tree of life and shake it until the fruit falls.

Finding today different from yesterday can be very difficult, especially for people who are trapped in menial jobs and who live in limited circumstances on low income, which is where most people live. The same old typewriter, the same old desk, the same drab office, the same four walls; we are caught in a deadly monotony. No time or money for vacations, no new faces, no different scenery, our lives slip farther and farther away from the vitality and hope of our youth.

If we aren't careful, we cross a certain line of doom, and from that time forward, we live in the land of the broken spirit. It is a strange land in which the older we get the more like ourselves

7

we become. If we are dependent, we grow more dependent, if cross then more cross, if complacent then more complacent, and if retreating, more retreating. People who have crossed that line of doom have completely ignored their inner impulse to creativity. They say: "Yes, I have had it. This is all there is to life for me!"

For years a man has worked on an assembly line fastening radiators to automobile frames. His sole task consists of lowering a radiator into place and tightening the bolt on his side of the car. Day in and day out, the same monotonous task, no joy, no variety, no freedom of expression. There are two ways open to him.

One is to squeeze his whole life into that one little bolt and to see it as a funnel through which he was pouring his vitality and existence. Each day more empty than the day before, he finally thinks of himself as the bolt. Take away the bolt and his life disappears.

The other way is to see the bolt as one part of a full life. He is not the bolt, but a complicated human being sensitive to the colors, the noise, the moving machinery, and the people all about him. His true work is not simply to instal radiators; rather it is life in touch with all the other manifestations of life. The time he spends at the assembly line is only a portion of the life he lives in creative contact with other life. He does not surrender to the meanness of his task, but he looks upon it as one of the faces of life among many other faces that are at the same time confronting him and asking him for his time and interest.

Some would say that the first way makes better cars, but I doubt this. Squeezed into that bolt, the workman becomes a dead man, and dead men don't build good cars. The best cars are built by men sensitive to the unending varieties of life all about them. To use the language of modern youth, they are "turned on."

Turning on is to become sensitive to the variety and challenge of life. It is to respond to the colors, the sounds, the shapes, and the textures of things that surround us. It is also to see and to feel the glory and the diversity of human beings as they come within reach of our eyes, our ears, and our love. It is to become aware of the salt and pepper variety of God's infinite creation and to accept life as an adventure into new relationships and new situations.

Turning on is to recapture beauty for the human eye, poetry for the human spirit, and God for the human soul. It is to live creatively, knowing that each day will bring some new experiences. It is to live expectantly, knowing that no matter how drab the colors may seem, it is God's plan that tomorrow they shall be brighter.

My childhood was blessed with the close friendship of a woman whose whole life was lived in response to the community to whom she was given by the hand of God. Mary Cree Cosby was an artist who painted hundreds of pictures in her fourscore years. Her home was one great house of color. Yet her greatest paintings were the lives in which she invested her friendship. Her best gift was her inspiration. Through her eyes and words, one could see and feel things he never experienced before.

Once on a long drive in our drab winter countryside, I commented on the dulness of the dead trees and the dried grass. "No, my young friend," she said. "Just look, don't you see the purple in that gray sky, and don't you see the deep blue of those distant woods and the yellow in that dried grass? Look, there is a bird's nest in that tree, and see how graceful are the limbs of the winter elm."

She created in me that day something I will never lose, but she created much more as I observed her faithful Christian service to the whole town. No matter how dirty the workman on the street, he was "Mister Jones," a person she could respect for some quality of goodness or greatness that she saw which others could not see. No matter how unpromising a child—and I was the most unpromising—she could find a small corner in which to grow confidence. Mary Cree Cosby was a short, round little woman, almost changeless in her appearance for her whole lifetime. She was just as constant in her zest for life. In her eightieth year she stood on my back porch and pointed to things of beauty I had never seen before. She died at the end of a sight-seeing vacation to the mountains of Colorado. Mary Cree Cosby was creative in the lives of others because she herself had submitted her whole life to the creative hands of God. She was truly turned on.

But we must not let the Mary Cree Cosbys of our lives trap us into the assumption that only the artists are creative. We must also avoid the assumption that true creativity is the making of some idea or article that the world has never seen before. This would deny to most people the joy of creativity, for there are not many artists and even fewer absolutely original people.

Common creativity, the kind we can all experience, can be applied to the growth and the development of life. It can help us find true joy and true happiness. And it can help us meet each new day with a prayer of thanksgiving for its opportunities are the kind that lead to great living. One of Mrs. Cosby's friends said of her: "She would have been a great woman had she never painted a picture, because she had learned how to successfully meet the challenges of life."

Let's face it, most people will never produce a line of writing or drawing worth preserving in museums. Even those in whom the drive is deepest and who finally succeed in the eyes of the world, will devise little of lasting beauty. Not one tenth of one percent of all the people will invent anything or compose any music. Most of what is invented and composed will be finally lost. Yet all of these people must keep on trying to add what beauty they can to the world.

Christian creativity is not something that we produce for ourselves. It is not salvation by works, a kind of substitute for surrender to God. Too many people make it this. In fact one would assume from the time and strength many people devote to their own special skills that what they make or do is a daily sacrifice laid on the altar of salvation and that the size and perfection of the sacrifice determine the amount of the salvation. Some people even work at religion like this. They act as though all power belonged to them and none to God.

True creativity in a Christian sense derives from a partnership with God. It admits willingly that for the person the first great act of creativity is man's own special spiritual re-creation. He is born again. This comes through his absolute surrender to the force which is to remake him. The second great act of personal creativity is man's awareness that he is truly a partner of God. "For we are his workmanship, created in Christ Jesus unto good works" (Eph. 2:10). The only way one can ever learn to live creatively with the monotony of modern life, its machines and its routine, is through a surrender to the wellspring of all creativity, to God himself. In him one will find the light of life that truly turns him on. He will find the secret for making each new day an adventure into the unknown and each new hour an encounter with some new reality.

It is one thing to say all this, it is another thing to prove it. Christians have been often told lately that too much of their preaching has been without proof. Perhaps our hearers do not understand the nature of our proof. The validity of Christian witness can be verified only as new believers discover it for themselves in their own lives. The demand for a rational proof of Christianity cuts squarely across the nature of Christianity itself. Christianity is a religion of faith, not of logic. It requires a heroic assumption that God is real and that he is always coming to man in Christ Jesus. There are three simple steps that can help us understand and act on this assumption and in this way enter into a creative partnership with God.

We must take God at his word when he says he wants to make something out of us. From the beginning God has been trying to get man's attention. He wants man to see that he is not his enemy. His word spoken to Abraham is his word spoken to the whole human race. "Fear not, Abram: I am thy shield, and thy exceeding great reward" (Gen. 15:1). It is as if he said, "Abraham, you are to have what you never had before."

This forward look for life is seen in the ministry and teachings of Jesus. He told his disciples: "I am come that they might have life, and that they might have it more abundantly" (John 10:10). He does his best to get men to live their lives in terms of their fullest possibilities. His use of parables from so many sources was one way he had of getting men to see the totality of life and their involvement in it. Look at the lilies of the field, he said, and look at the birds of the air. Look at the trees and the mountains, look at the leaven in the meal.

The abundant life is the creative life; it comes in response to our awareness of God's marvelous world. It comes also in our response to his life-giving promises. "I am the vine, ye are the branches. He that abideth in me, and I in him, the same bringeth forth much fruit: for without me ye can do nothing" (John 15:5). It is not the will of God that we be snatched out of the world, isolated from its beauties and its wonders. In fact, it is his will that we *not* be snatched from the world. He wants us to take our place in the midst of his creation, yet not as ordinary people, but as fruit bearers. He recognizes that our relationship to him in a sense alienates us from the world. "I have chosen you out of the world, therefore the world hateth you" (John 15:19). Yet we are to live out our lives as members of an alien community.

This tension is the tension of divine creativity, like that which Jesus himself felt on his last journey to Jerusalem. He knew what he faced, but he would not withdraw from it. It was the tension that pulled him toward the cross and set him plainly before the whole world as God's greatest creative act. It was the tension for which the promises of God prepared him, a tension he could endure because he knew "all things that the Father hath are mine" (John 16:15).

God's creative drive in which he takes the dull and the luster-less, the unpromising and the undeserving, the inept and the lifeless, the untalented and the ignorant, the poor and the dropouts, and makes them into kings and queens and turns their eyes in the direction of faith and hope has another name. It is "amazing grace."

It cannot be simulated by good works or even bad works, for what happens in our own strength and of our own hands lacks the divine fire of life. Man, by his own lifting may climb a little higher than his fellows, but only as he is a new creation of God can his life become eternal. It is from grace "not your own doing, it is the gift of God" (Eph. 2:8, RSV). It is an experience that comes only to those who would dare to lean on the promises of God.

We must learn through faith to tap the resources of God. This is an old, old refrain. Every Christian since the disciples has sung it, but it must be sung again, for it is the truth. If we are to meet life as a challenge and find answers to its problems; if we are to add something to this world's store of faith and hope and if we are to take our places as molders of a better tomorrow, it comes down to one thing—whatever strength and leverage we possess must be augmented by the strength and leverage of God.

Man truly must learn to lean on God. He must literally be removed from himself. He must put forth his hand into the dark and grasp what he cannot see or understand. Whatever new thing he draws back from the dark he must use as the gift of God, to mold and to make his life into something new. The reaching itself is a part of the creative process, for in it man is acknowledging that within himself he is not sufficient, and that his life must be added to, if he is to grow and to cope with his challenge.

Whatever you become as you claim God's resources, you become in fulfilment of God's dream for you. It is the realization of God's idea of your personality. One of the strongest and most vibrant men I ever knew had one of the frailest bodies. Paroxysms of unrelenting pain and periods of overwhelming weakness never kept him from appearing always to be something above and beyond his body. He never seemed to succumb in spirit to his suffering. He had learned to tap God's resources for the strength he needed.

Man cannot draw from his own being the raw materials needed for the transformation of his personality. Even if he had a proper bucket and let it down inside himself, he would draw up nothing. These are times when he may appear to be drawing from himself, but even then he is drawing from the great chasm of his experiences, not of himself, but of himself in touch with all the world. As a person, an entity separate from God, he is still dependent on God for the raw materials of his life. The resources of God, whether God's own Spirit or the things God had made, provide man the raw products and the power of his own creation.

Jesus asked the woman of Samaria for a drink. She chided him for being a Jew and making the request of her. He said: "If you only knew what God gives, and who it is that is asking you for a drink, you would have asked him and he would have given you living water" (John 4:10, TEV). The woman was dependent, but she did not know she was dependent. Until she was willing to put aside herself and to draw with humility from the depths of God, she could not find the resources for re-creation. Her problem was to be true to herself and to find her true self. She had the choice of two attitudes: defiance and humility.

The wisdom of this world would tell her to take the way of defiance. "Express yourself," it says. "Let yourself go. Withdraw from others. Be an individual." The Christian way is the way of humility. "Surrender" it says. "Except a corn of wheat fall into the ground and die, it abideth alone, but if it die, it bringeth forth much fruit. He that loveth his life shall lose it, and he that hateth his life in this world shall keep it unto life eternal." The only way we can find ourselves is to sacrifice ourselves. Humility is leaning on God's resources.

Jesus also told of the three men given different sums of money. The two with the larger sums did well and returned to their master with handsome profits. The man with the least amount buried his in the ground and returned empty-handed. Nicolas Berdyaev says that gifts are from God and indicate that man is intended to do creative work. Burying one's personal talents in the ground is a denial of the manifestation of God in his life. The presence of talent is the challenge to creativity. But as I have already said, creativity must not be thought of only as some work of art. To really become, man must think of himself as something still being made. God supplies the possibilities; man takes the initiative.

So far, in our quest for the re-created life we have seen two things. To be truly re-created one must accept God at his word, and he must lean upon his resources. The third is just as important.

If we are to be truly creative, we must find ourselves in God. The plea we often hear for men to find themselves, to learn who they are and why they exist is not merely a fadish injunction of modern psychology. It is an idea as old as Socrates who said: "Know thyself." Indeed it is as old as Job who said: "What is man, that thou shouldest magnify him?" (Job 7:17). Man has always puzzled over himself. Moses, when challenged with a call to go to Egypt and deliver the children of Israel, replied: "Who am I, that I should go unto Pharaoh?" (Ex. 3:11).

Most of the time man does not puzzle over himself in awareness of God's presence, and this is his undoing. His lack of awareness of the Eternal leads him to false starts and to paths that go down to the grave with life unrequited. The world tells him, "Be yourself," and usually this means to throw off the constraint of the Eternal God. "God is an inhibition that thrusts and limits. You are not really free until you are free of God." With words like these the world pushes God into limbo. It claims that the ultimate freedom is for one to be able to disown the last controlling influence of life. It assumes that this is the way for persons to truly know and be themselves.

But how wrong the world is in this! The only way a man can

know his world is by the light of the sun. Even if man travels at night, he is guided by the light of the moon which is reflected sunlight or he finds his way with an electric lamp which is stored up sunlight. The figure of darkness is used in the New Testament to depict the lostness of man. Jesus said that "he that walketh in darkness knoweth not whither he goeth" (John 12:35). John said: "God is light, and in him is no darkness" (1 John 1:5). Paul said that it is Christ who "delivered us from the power of darkness" (Col. 1:13). The only way a man can know his true self is by the light of God.

When Jesus told Simon Peter that he was a pile of sand and that he wanted to make a rock out of him, he was not merely changing Peter, though there was considerable change involved. He was drawing out Simon Peter's character, extricating it from sin and conformity. He was leading Peter into his own uniqueness as a person. Before the experience Peter was like a thousand other fishermen, vain, profane, earthy, violent, impulsive. Afterward, he was himself a molder and maker of men, a prophet and a martyr, a man unique among all men. The difference was his creative experience of God in Christ.

A man must be himself. He must live his own life and make his own decisions. He cannot become an authentic creative individual except his will be actively consenting to the teaching of his experience. Truly, one cannot "learn" another person something he knows. Perhaps one cannot even teach him, unless there is consent to learning. Creative teaching is knowing precisely where and how one's own experience can mesh with another's experience and will to effect discovery of new insights and values. I put it like this to show that creative becoming is not something a father imposes on his son, but something the son discovers from his experiences. It is not something God imposes, but something we discover from communion with God.

Creative becoming is dependent of three things: growth, self-confidence and freedom. If Simon Peter was to become the rock, he had to be given an opportunity to develop, had to keep his self-confidence and had to feel unthreatened as a person. On first glance, one would assume that in his surrender to Jesus all of these were destroyed. This is what the world thinks, but it is exactly opposite the truth. Jesus came to give more light, not less; freedom indeed, not mere freedom. In him the mustard seed becomes the tree, the leaven the meal, the grain of wheat the mighty stalk. When Simon was self-confident enough to attempt to walk on the water, Jesus lifted him into the boat. When he felt threatened and intimidated, Jesus said: "Feed my sheep."

We can all be immitators of Jesus in helping in the life formation of others, but we had better keep in mind some principles that Jesus appeared to have in mind. One of these was that he always creates the new man in keeping with that man's general life style. To his dying day Simon was still Simon, not Paul, not John. God rarely calls any person to work beyond the sphere of his natural interests and abilities. Another principle was that Jesus always had a profound respect for Simon Peter as a person. Looking at the relationships of the two, I do not see any signs of domination. Jesus did not force Simon or confute him or deceive him. Jesus was quite content to accept him as an imperfect person, knowing that a piece of burned cloth or a broken stick has values. Still another, Jesus always looked beneath the surface to see the real man. He did not project on Simon Peter his image of John the Baptist or of any other person. He was quite willing for Simon to develop as his own man. Finally, Jesus was always careful to maintain spontaneity. Spontaneity is the natural condition of growth. Without it nothing can abound. In my backyard there is a ten-year-old boxwood not twelve inches high. It has been pruned and fertilized and transplanted; sprayed and mulched, given sunlight and shade, protected from bicycles and dogs, begged and entreated, yet stubbornly it lives but does not grow. I can only conclude that somehow it has been denied spontaneity. The bursting, tumbling creative life processes are not present. The boxwood languishes under the oppression of too much attention.

This vignette of Simon Peter illustrates the creative relationship of Jesus Christ to every man. He tries to draw us out of our bondage to self, without destroying our personality. He points out a path for us, and he expects us to walk in it on our own. He opens our eyes wide to the wonders of his creation, and asks us to look for ourselves. He warns but he does not threaten. He expects us to try, but he lifts us up when our efforts fail. He takes interest in what we do, but he is more interested in who we are. He calls us servants, but he treats us like kings and queens. He offers himself as the way, the truth, and the light, but he compels no man to walk in it against his will. He offers himself as the bread and water of life, but none are to eat and drink except they choose.

This open spontaneous relationship is the divine milieu of God's creative reformation of man. It is the area in which darkness and light are fighting over the dignity and the destiny of man. It is the glorious unfolding, the great making, the re-creation in which the first Adam created in the image of God and given his breath, is re-created in the second Adam and given his Spirit. It is God taking nothing and making something out of it, the gift eternal, amazing grace.

This relationship of God to man in Christ is the supremely creative experience for man. It is his everlasting turning on.

CHAPTER 2

Creative Worship

■ ■ ■

Man's selfish inward looking at himself makes him a monster. He soon becomes the biggest thing on his own horizon. As he grows important in his own eyes, he becomes fat and sensuous. He is gorged with food, decorated with ornaments, surrounded with all the things that make life soft and easy. He becomes more like himself, deceitful, devious, blind and grotesque. His worship of himself "de-creates" him into something less than the image of God. He stands exactly where Adam stood the day he took his eyes off God and looked at the apple.

In that pristine shift of attention man the eternal became man the finite. He became what he looked at. It is sad but true that if a man looks long enough at himself he will come to see nothing but a glob of corruption filled with worms, for as a physical self that is his end. He sees what he becomes, and he becomes what he sees.

On the other hand, if he gazes beyond himself, man also becomes what he sees. The greater his wonder and awe, the more amazing his own personal development. If he looks far enough and if he looks in the right place, he becomes a king, a kind of an eternal king belonging to the ages.

Of course, he can look in the wrong place and in the wrong way and become a puppet, which is precisely what so many people of our times have done. They settle for a mechanistic view of life and end up as sticks in a tinker-toy windmill. They have plenty of wonder and awe, but at the end is blind chance. They see all nature in impersonal scientific terms and themselves as merely another equation in the formula of change, a blob of nothing, with no one out there to contemplate them, a piece of dust to be blown in the cosmic winds, a fragment of the stars, a really meaningless moment of existence, an accident of time, an absolute nothing. Man can get awfully little and terribly despondent thinking about himself a part of a mechanistic order. He worships all right, but his worship ends in futility. There is nothing in it that adds to his own dignity and destiny.

It is important that we look with wonder and awe far enough and in the right place. True worship is the kind that turns the eyes of man toward One who is life himself, toward the Person above all other persons, toward him who contemplates the creature and takes pride in what he has made and given breath too, toward God, the eternal, the rewarder of them that diligently seek him.

Poor stumbling man has a way of missing the obvious, and his conviction of the nature of ultimate reality proves this. He worships the moon and spends vast sums trying to reach it. He worships science and prostitutes himself to its premises. He worships a golden calf and pours his riches into it. Man is not moon dust, nor is he an algebraic formula, nor a gold coin. He may contain gold in his body and perhaps a little dust, for all I know, and he may be reduced to a formula, but he is none of these things. Man is personality, and that says a lot about the nature of ultimate reality.

As a thinking, feeling, remembering, value-conscious personality, I cannot buy the assumption of science that existence is totally mechanistic. To me, the obvious thing is not that the body is a balanced formula of salt water and a few other combinations of elements, and therefore God is not. No, emphatically not. The obvious thing is that man is personality and therefore God must be personal. "I am" therefore "God is!"

To look at God with wonder and awe is to look far enough

and to look in the right place. It is the only kind of looking that will give man the understandings of himself that he should have. If I look at myself, I become a pile of worms; if I look at the mechanistic order, I become an algebraic formula. If I look at God, I become a person of dignity, capable of eternal growth.

It took me a long time to see that most of us find the wrong interpretation on the question of the psalmist: "What is man, that thou art mindful of him?" (Ps. 8:4). The point is not that man is a dreg at the bottom of the cup which God discovers and tolerates? It is not that man is a worm in the dust or a mote in in the eye of God. This would have been to say that man is not really important, and may have been the way David viewed it. But this is not the way it turns out in the New Testament. From the point of view of Jesus, man is important. He is the lost son, the lost sheep, the lost coin. He is not ashamed to call them brethren and he tasted death for everyone of them. Moreover, he wants to make them into priests and kings.

True worship of God then is an act of primary creativity. Just about the first thing it does is to help man see himself in the perspective of the eternal. It also renews his self-confidence and opens the way to spontaneity. It says that man was meant for growth, and that the starting point is a sense of well-being in God's presence.

The atheists have condemned worship as a human creation of a god who devours man or one who favors himself with lavish praise. These men miss the point of worship altogether. In worship God is not seeking man for himself but offering himself to man. God is not the insatiable ego looking for the praise of his creatures. He is not a sponge that feeds himself on incense and tears. The New Testament refutes this pagan idea of God. From our early Christian witness we learn that God does not take away, but gives. He does not destroy, but builds up. He does not cut himself away from man, but ties himself to man. He is not the golden calf, but the loving father. He is not the deaf ear, but the eternal Word.

Worship puts man in touch with reality. Indeed, true worship is to establish reality. Once on a train in the night I stood in the vestibule marveling at the crushing sound of steel against steel. Suddenly the whole world vanished and I had a sense of being involved in that noise. I could not tell whether reality lay where I was or back in Fort Worth at the seminary. So overwhelming was my involvement in the sound and my sense of detachment from the world that for days I lived with the experience as a kind of ghost that carried me back and forth between two questions: "Who am I?" and "Why am I?" I have never been able to figure out what there was in that sound that triggered so much emotion and introspection.

In those days I went about with a constant prayer on my lips: "O God, thy will be done." It was a period of great doubt and great belief. Life was a constant stretching for experience and insight. This may seem strange to you, but I have come to believe that in that moment on the old Rock Island train in the middle of the night between Fort Worth and Bowie, in the sound of that clashing steel I had a worship experience. Reality was neither in the world or in the sound. It was in God who set me thinking anew: Who am I? and Why am I? My prayer was being answered with a new experience and a new insight. I was growing. Ultimate reality had come to me in a common everyday experience.

The trouble with our experience with God is that we just don't look for him in enough different places. We shut him up behind the huge doors of our churches and leave him there from one Sunday to another. We go back every week to what we pedantically call "a worship experience" as though God were so formal as to keep appointments with us by the clock and in certain places. I don't want to be misunderstood here, for I emphatically believe in worship Sunday morning, Sunday night, and Wednesday night with my brethren in the church house. Moreover I believe in attendance checks and record keeping. I've got a lifelong record that proves this. I would like it just as clear, however, that I believe that our concept of such services as exclusive "worship experiences" is precisely why God seems so unreal to so many people. Reality cannot be confined to a church house.

If God is reality, he can be found present in all kinds of experiences at all kinds of times. He comes to us when we least expect him, speaking in tongues most strange. Not long ago in mowing the grass I discovered something I should have known before: Wild strawberries were growing in my yard. I was amazed to see tiny hard strawberries, bright and red, growing beneath the top of the grass. For years I had noticed in the spring that when I walked about the yard my shoes would sometimes be faintly marked with red stain. As I looked at my discovery, the thought came to me that here God is, under my feet, growing a thing of beauty and wonder. At sunset I showed the strawberries to my wife. Carefully she picked a dozen of the tiny fruit and their leaves and took them in the house and arranged them as a bouquet in a Chinese spoon on our kitchen table. That was amazing. Reality had come into the house and was celebrated as a thing of beauty.

For me, this is the order of worship: the constant discovery of God's presence in the everyday experiences of life and the celebration of these experiences in the church house. This is the order that leads to the acceptance of God as reality. It is quite a different thing from the concept that many hold that God as reality is discovered in the church house and somehow transported to the world. To me the difference between the two is the difference between a religious God and a secular God. Too long the world has viewed God as a religious God. He is confined to a temple and is sitting on a throne. This is the concept Jesus wanted to destroy. For him God is the God secular. He is to be found in the world. He reaches out after man through parables and through spiritual experiences. He is not on a throne but on a cross, and he is in the world, for at the death of Christ the veil of the Temple was torn from top to bottom, and

God stepped out into the world. The temple has become the meeting-house and God is there by appointment for those people who greeted him in the noise of trains and the marvels of wild strawberries.

There are people reading this who will say: "What nonsense!" they don't believe in the God of wild strawberries and roaring trains. They don't believe in God at all. They think such things are superstition and fancy tales. Their idea of ultimate reality is what can be deposited in a bank. They can make a real good case for their position. But what happens when their eyes go blind, or their bodies get so cold that there is not enough feeling in their fingers to enable them to button their buttons, or when the bank goes broke. At the end of all such concepts of reality is failure because the human processes on which they are based ultimately fail. They are all dependent on what man can do.

I like my concept of reality better. God does not fail when I fail, or weaken when I weaken, or die when I die. He lives, speaking in personal terms to man, one generation after another. He comes to me in the little boy Jesus, from the agony of Gethsemane, from the fierce suffering of Golgotha, and from the joy of the empty tomb. He comes from the lilies of the field, the falling sparrows, the fig tree by the wayside, the grapevine in the vineyard, and the wine in the communion glass.

The men who fight this kind of reality remind me of a poor woman I knew long ago who claimed to be an infidel. She fought the church and all it stood for, proclaiming it as unreal and superstition. I used to go see her just to hear her talk about her infidelity. Usually she would drift around to talking about the strange people who lived in her house. She never saw them, she said. But they lived there in the attic, in the chimney and in the water heater. Some of them helped her, some tormented her, but she found them a lot of company. We finally had to put that woman in the asylum. About that same time our church had a prayer vigil. I came on two of our ladies praying together in the church. As I watched them, a strange contrast came into mind, the poor demented woman talking to the voices of the chimney and water heater, my faithful friends talking to God. The difference is the listening on the other end of the line. The woman talking to the water heater went further and further from sanity, the women talking to God became more and more sane. One was moving toward insanity being "de-created" from what reality she had; the others were moving toward sanity, being created unto a greater and greater reality.

Worship is a kind of life journey, in which we are transformed from grace unto grace, by faith unto faith, through the atoning power of Christ Jesus. Every step is a step of growing assurance and increasing reality.

Worship makes the most of your life. When Jesus walked with his disciples through the cornfield on the sabbath, he plucked a grain of wheat and began to eat it. The Pharisees were horrified and condemned him for violating the law of the sabbath. Jesus then pointed out a principle that puts man and God into new relationship to each other. He simply said that the sabbath was made for man and not man for the sabbath.

The Pharisees could not understand that a law made to honor God could turn into a law destructive to man. They would have man serve God solely for God's sake. Jesus taught us that there is an added dimension. Yes, man does serve God for God's sake; yet man also serves God for his own sake. Who has not seen this in the New Testament has missed one of its cardinal lessons. The famous statement of the Scottish Shorter Catechism puts this idea poetically: "The chief end of man is to glorify God, and to enjoy Him forever."

Some of our dour legalistic Christian fathers glorified God without finding pleasure in him. They had tied themselves up into all kinds of laws and regulations to keep them from enjoying his marvelous world. Too many present-day Christians still believe this, else they would not leave God locked up in the church house all week long.

True worship enables you to grow and develop as a human

being as well as a child of God. Joseph Goldbruner, a Christian psychologist said: "Every individual represents a creative idea of God." [1] Myself as a creative idea of God means that like the tulip bulb I planted yesterday, there is in my nature a pattern toward which I can develop. There is something I can become. Everything I do is a step toward the unfolding of that pattern. Sometimes I move consciously as if inspired by the pattern in full view. Most of the time I move subconsciously, not realizing what it is I am moving toward. The important thing is to move in freedom. Yes, to move in freedom, that is the secret.

Most people do not move in freedom for they are bound to sin. They are chained to sin and the law. Sometimes they enter deeply into sin in the name of freedom, not realizing that sin ties them with fine wires which grow to be great cables. The heaviest load they carry is their unforgiven sin. Even for Christians, the weight of sin is heavy, because they have not learned that forgiveness is a continuing experience which must be consciously entered into. They forgot their prayer: "Forgive us our debts, as we have also forgiven our debtors" (Matt. 6:12, RSV).

Some of us do move in freedom toward God's idea of ourselves. We have found the liberating secret and are being molded into "the image of his Son" (Rom. 8:29). We participate in the divine tension between the completeness of God's idea for us and the perfection of ourselves in Christ. This tension that shapes and forms our spiritual being is fully as marvelous as the womb that formed our physical being. This drawing together of our essential selves with the recreating power of Christ is our reborning. It is the magnificent process of all things becoming new in him.

To achieve this liberation, life itself must become worship. The conversion experience is the first step toward life becoming worship. Saying an emphatic no to sin and a believing yes to Christ is to accept eternal life. We make an irrevocable contract. From that point our fulfilment depends on how well we give ourselves to that contract. Paul spoke, putting the challenge bluntly: "So then, my brothers, because of God's many mercies to us, I make this appeal to you: Offer yourselves as a living sacrifice to God, dedicated to his service and pleasing to him. This is the true worship that you should offer" (Rom. 12:1, TEV). It is the holy giving of ourselves to God, the unstinted surrender of the will, the determination not just to pray but to live the life of prayer. It is not saccharine talk about how much you love the Lord, and it is not a sanctimonious air. It is not even praying over food in a public place—though I am not against that, but it is a quiet determination to live everyday in the will and spirit of Jesus Christ. It even means that you may recoil on hearing the meeting place of Christians referred to as the sanctuary, for in true worship you will have discovered that every place is a sanctuary where God is to be honored. It means most of all that you are caught up in a great unifying force, one that gives you more and more sanity, more and more integrity and more and more completeness. It means you will be precisely what God meant you to be—yourself. It means you will be *real.*

Ancient Greek actors wore masks through which they spoke their parts. These were called *personas.* We wear *personas,* sometimes dozens of them, to hide the reality of ourselves. Jesus Christ wants to help us get rid of our personas. As long as we use them, there is no freedom. They even drive us mad. The Gadarene madman spoke a multitude of voices. He was many men, and not one of them himself. The terror of his plight is seen in the act of Jesus in transferring these mad voices to the pigs which immediately went mad and jumped into the sea. If a confusion of voices drives insensitive pigs mad, what do they do to sensitive men?

We can all look back to outstanding moments of worship. Those we remember are the ones most formative in our lives. They are the experiences of great personal creation, and mark turning points in personality and habits. In my early youth I had two such experiences that left me with a sense of special dependence on God.

One Sunday afternoon I walked through the woods to a hill-top ringed with a thicket of post oak trees. It made a good pray-ing place, and I had a problem to solve. The ground was covered with rocks, and almost without thinking I began to pick up them and form great letters. By nightfall I had handled just about every rock in that clearing and had built a huge sentence that read: "The greatest thing a young man can do is to give his life to God." As the evening shadows fell and the cold winds blew, I knelt in the midst of my little creation and gave myself anew to Christ. I cannot think of that hour without a sense of awe. The awe, however, is not in the rocky hilltop. The cows have long ago kicked my little monument to pieces. Shinnery and prickle pear have just about covered the clearing. The awe is not there, only nostalgia. But every time I look within my heart I find that experience a bulwark against a wavering faith and a dimming hope. I find awe within, a reminder that I wor-shiped and from God I received strength that will never die and vision that will never perish.

Another time on another hilltop, I took an old trunk key and carved the same words into sandstone. Just at sunset the clouds parted and I stood for a brief moment in the sunlight. The soft brass key was worn to a splinter and I was tired, but not too tired to make the decision I knew I must make, to leave Texas and go to Oklahoma. It turned out to be the pivotal decision of my life, and I've always had a certain amount of confidence in the fact that I made it in worship while I worked away on that sandstone. When the sun had set, I walked into the shadowy valley and up the road to the church house. God walked with me, not in the gravel but in my inner life. I met him at the sand-stone altar, and he left with me to help me fight the battle of change. Since then they have moved the road and destroyed the hill, but the place does not matter, as much as I would like to see it. What does matter is that I worshiped and God created in me a little more strength and vision with which to face the future. What I received from him moves me toward the completeness that I am to someday have in him.

In closing this chapter I would like to quote a passage from Josef Goldbrunner: "God, the All-Holy, is freely flowing and flourishing Life. He is whole; there is no blemish of disease in Him, no poison of death. In Him lies our health and salvation; in His nearness is healing for body and soul. The striving after the Godlike makes for health and wholeness. The more we seek the perfection that makes man like God, that makes him holy, the more we should become healthy in body and soul, for holiness is health." [2] The point of this quotation is that God whom we seek in worship, is the God who can and will create us as the best possible person under all circumstances. To worship him is to be created to the holiness that is wholeness. God has decreed worship, not for his own satisfaction, but for man's edification.

NOTES

1. Josef Goldbruner, *Cure of Mind and Cure of Soul* (Notre Dame: The University of Notre Dame Press, 1962) p. 41.

2. Josef Goldbruner, Holiness in Wholeness (Notre Dame: The University of Notre Dame Press, 1964) p. 1.

CHAPTER 3

Creative Witness

■ ■ ■

A very young minister waited for a friend in an airport terminal. Not wanting to waste time, he read his church magazines and when he left he put them in a tract box of another denomination. He thought—or perhaps he didn't think—In this way I will put my truth alongside their error. Almost instantly he forgot about his innocent little strategem. A few days later he answered the telephone. An airline pilot was at the other end, and as the man talked the young minster began to realize that his strategem was not as innocent as he thought. The pilot said, "I fly in and out of a great many airports and in several of them I have installed tract boxes. My Christian vocation is to keep them filled with literature from my church. My odd flying hours make it impossible for me to attend my church regularly, but I can do this in answer to the call of God. Now, will you respect my vocation by providing yourself with a pamphlet box of your own?" The young minister apologized.

This brings us to two questions basic for the Christian: What is Christian witness? and, What is creative Christian witness? The serious Christian who has truly committed his life to Christ will think about these questions until he answers them himself.

What is Christian witness? For the airline pilot it may have been simply to keep the pamphlet boxes filled. If that was all, then he had a much limited conception. Surely there is more to witness than a few simple gestures of faithfulness.

Witness is not one act or one word. It is not even a series of acts or words. These are important parts of witness, but by no means are they the whole of witness. Witness of the kind that Jesus had in mind is total life commitment. It is the irrevocable promise, the uncompromising vocation, the relentless struggle. One could keep all the pamphlet boxes filled and still miss the mark. One might even appear to be a life-giving witness and be nothing but an empty shell. In fact, no person can be certain of himself being a true witness until the end when he hears his Lord say: "Be thou faithful unto death, and I will give thee a crown of life" (Rev. 2:10). A true witness does not take pride in himself as a true witness. He knows that pride in spiritual matters is a sure way to slam the door against the Holy Spirit.

None of this is meant to set aside as unnecessary or unimportant the daily works of witness. After all the pamphlet boxes are extremely important; yet not as the actual witness but as evidence of the witness. A close study of the New Testament shows that there can be many daily works which will help establish one's testimony for the kingdom of God. They are to be taken seriously as a challenge to the Christian life.

Proclamation or preaching as we often call it is a foundational witness. Indeed much of the witness of the New Testament is proclamation of the resurrection of Christ as one of the central facts of the gospel. Preaching seems so foolish to those who do not understand the nature of the gospel and the truth of the New Testament. In times of falling away, Christians tend to de-emphasize preaching, substituting for it all kinds of good works. Paul warned: "For the preaching of the cross is to them that perish foolishness" (1 Cor. 1:18).

Once on a New York subway train I saw an old man with a megaphone and a Bible reading aloud to those that set around him. Edging closer I began to question him.

"What are you doing?"

"I am shouting the gospel," he answered.

"Why do you do this?"

"It is my calling."

I watched him a long time. Some of the people listened. Some sat indifferent. A few sophisticated folk laughed at him. One man in a clergy collar frowned and moved to the other end of the car. This simple shouter's calling is not my calling but as a preacher from a pulpit am I any less rejected by the world? Certainly not, for to the world preaching is always a foolish thing. It is nevertheless vital, something I must always do, and something from which I cannot escape. As a witness for Christ I have an obligation to participate in the witness of preaching. But I must not fall into the trap of thinking that proclamation is the only kind of witness.

Good works are also a witness. Jesus put it very simply: "Let your light so shine before men, that they may see your good works, and glorify your father which is in heaven" (Matt. 5:16). Good works are meaningless unless they are related to the preaching of the gospel. Preaching without good works is sterile and ineffective. When I think of good works, I think of one of the great Christian women of my experience, a spinster who was devoutly loved by her whole church because of her constant good works. Catherine Oman loved people and followed Jesus Christ. She headed the Extension department and carried in her heart a hundred people for whom she found ways of doing immeasurable good deeds. Like a true Christian, she ministered to all classes, the rich as well as the poor. She could not teach for an accident had deprived her of her voice. During her last years she could not drive her car, but she found ways to work through others. On Sundays when life was waning she would simply sit in a pew and minister to people who came to speak to her. Good works were the natural instinct of her Christian life. She made her Christian witness wherever she happened to be. One friend said of her: "I knew her for fifty years and she always seems to represent the life and character of Jesus Christ to me."

The personal word is a vital way of Christian witness. Sometimes this is the only way people will really hear. If one is truly a Christian, he will find his own way to speak positively for Jesus Christ, but he will speak, and his speaking will be effective, for the ministry of personal words is one that the Holy Spirit always honors. One lasting impression left me by my grandfather was the way he made his personal witness. A frontier farmer who had to retire from the farm at seventy-two because of a broken hip, he built a small service station and grocery store. When a stranger stopped for gasoline, my grandfather would engage him in conversation mostly about the weather and the crops, but he would always shift around to the question, "Are you a Christian man?" He never failed to gently impress on the stranger the need for Christian decision. His was the direct approach.

The indirect approach in the use of the personal word sometimes can be even more effective. Jesus used the indirect approach as much as the direct, frequently making his point with a parable, and sometimes with a question. He asked a woman, "Where is thine husband?" Sometimes he made a simple disarming statement like, "Let him that is without sin cast the first stone," or "Keep the commandments." Jesus did not, however, use the indirect method as an evasion or as apology—as many of us do. He never failed to press his point.

J. Howard Williams was one of the most disarming men when faithfully giving his Christian witness. Waitress, taxi driver, porters, policemen, lawyers, doctors—he always began where they were and worked through their hopes and dreams to confrontation for Christ. He was not abrupt or crude, and he worked as a good minister of Christ. Once I saw him speak to a stranger in front of a pawnshop. They were standing together looking at guns. I never knew when it happened, but in the end the man walked away with his whole life changed, still not realizing that God had come to him in the flaming fire of a personal word from a fellow human being. There was nothing haughty or proud or forbidding in Howard Williams. He never walked with any man except on the pathway of equality, and he never talked with any man without lifting him up.

Simple Christian being is perhaps the most far-reaching and effective way to witness. It is frequently discounted by persons who feel that the kingdom of God completely depends on the deeds of men. These critics say: "It is never enough for one simply to be a Christian. One must perform mighty works in order to show his power." In an activist age, such as ours, simple Christian being is interpreted as goodness for nothing. It is even criticized as a malign goodness that feeds on itself. One young critic said of church members: "All you people do is to get together in the church and love one another, while the world burns." Yes, the world is burning, but it just might be that simple Christian being is the best way to keep it from burning. It sometimes seems that the more people try to fix the world, the more it becomes unfixed.

The New Testament case for being is clear and consistent. The Beatitudes stress the need and reward for being.

> "How blest are those who know that they are poor; the kingdom of Heaven is theirs.
>
> How blest are the sorrowful; they shall find consolation.
>
> How blest are those of a gentle spirit; they shall have the earth for their possession.
>
> How blest are those who hunger and thirst to see right prevail; they shall be satisfied.
>
> How blest are those who show mercy; mercy shall be shown to them.
>
> How blest are those whose hearts are pure; they shall see God.
>
> How blest are the peacemakers; God shall call them his sons.
>
> How blest are those who have suffered persecution for the cause of right; the kingdom of Heaven is theirs."
>
> Matthew 5:3–10, NEB

Lives stamped with these words bear the hallmark of Christian quality and Christian quality is what the world needs. A little black boy ran from a white man. His mother asked,

"Robert, why did you run?" The boy instantly said, "I didn't know if he was a good man or not." All human beings are much the same. They will naturally suspect people who have not proved their goodness. One of these Beatitudes stands out in the minds of most people: "How blest are those of a gentle spirit; they shall have the earth for their possession" or as we have more often read it: "Blessed are the meek: for they shall inherit the earth" (Matt. 5:5). The whole world waits for the man of meekness in whom Christian being is the essence of life. Just who is this man of meekness? I will tell you.

> The man of meekness is firm without being hard.
> He is shrewd but not wily.
> He is strong but not destructive.
> He is intelligent but not overbearing.
> The man of meekness seeks no credit.
> He listens intensely with the heart.
> He asserts his love and even his ideas but not himself.
> When in trouble the man of meekness does not run.
> He does not create false issues or cast false images.
> He is no prima donna.
> He is not afraid of his enemies.
> He never builds himself up at the expense of others.
> He is never concerned with what he calls, "My rights."
> He makes no proud assertions.
> He does not contemplate his own meekness.
> He fights with words and ideas but not with doubts or slurs.
> He defends himself with true spirit and an open attitude but not with the destruction of others.
> He stands by his convictions and admires his enemies who stand by theirs.
> He pitches his battle on fair ground; if he loses, he asks no quarter; if he wins, he helps bind up the wounds of his enemy.
> None need fear losing anything to the man of meekness, neither purse, nor character, nor life.
> He sits at the foot of the table until he is asked to come higher.

He goes to the bottom of the line and spells his way to the
top, never boasting.
He is big enough to look any man in the eyes, but small
enough so no man has to look up to him.
To some he looks like a zero, to others a world of hope, a
world of wholeness, through whom the earth is about to be
reborn.

Creative Christian witness is a life-giving experience. A young
man wrote Dr. C. B. Jackson, a Texas evangelist who was most
unusually blessed with the gift of charisma: "What is the secret
of a successful revival meeting?" Dr. Jackson wrote in response
that great revivals are never contrived, but are the overflow of
the human experience with Christ. That same young man sat in
the study of Dr. Robert G .Lee and asked: "Dr. Lee, what is
the secret of your great success as an evangelist?" He talked at
length about how he studied and wrote out his sermons. The
young man interrupted: "Many men do that, yet they do not
have your gift." The great man hesitated a long time. When he
spoke it was with intense feeling: "Jesus is real to me. When I
preach, I am conscious of the multitudes, but I am much more
conscious of him. Sometimes he is so close I could touch him if
I dared." He then pointed to a painting of the humble country
home in which he was born. "There was my beginning. Anything I've been able to accomplish has not been anything I have
done, but what Christ has done through me." Another Texas
evangelist, Thomas J. Doss, a man of remarkable spiritual power
and insight once said: "God is most real to me in study and
prayer. Here something happens which is still happening when
I stand up to preach."

These testimonies show that the foundation of all witness is
an inner experience in which the reality of God's presence in
human life is irrevocably established. It is indeed the *irrevocable*
happening which started long ago when God began his movement toward man in Christ. It is a *reality* happening sealed in
the death of Christ on the cross, authenticated in the resurrec-

tion and made everywhere available in the advent of the Holy Spirit. It is a *koinonia* happening enriched throughout the ages by "a great cloud of witnesses" who poured their lives into it. It is a *spiritual* happening which cannot be proved by human logic or justified by human facts, and it comes only to men who are committed to it, always passing by those who try to find it by human wisdom, human desire, or human kinship. Indeed it is a *divine* happening, God's alone to give, a happening of grace imparted only to those who sincerely and honestly surrender to it. If one falls away, what happened was not the irrevocable happening, but a spurious substitution, and he is a cloud without rain, a tree without fruit, and a star without orbit. He is a dog returned to his own vomit and a Lot's wife turned into a pillar of salt. The irrevocable happening requires an irrevocable commitment. "Be thou faithful unto death, and I will give thee a crown of life" (Rev. 2:10).

Dr. Jackson's word "overflow" is the key to gracious witness. Not all people can be apostles and prophets. Paul makes this clear in his discourse on spiritual gifts: "And God hath set some in the church, first apostles, secondarily prophets, thirdly teachers, after that miracles, then gifts of healing, helps, governments, diversities of tongues" (1 Cor. 12:28). But all persons can be witnesses and can reflect mastery of the best gifts of all: faith, hope, and love. Only as these three gifts exist in human personality is there power for enduring creative witness. As preacher, I may be greatly concerned about my gestures and my diction, I may have precisely the right pulpit manner, and tell all the right illustrations. I may even master the latest 101 ways to give an invitation, but if I have not faith, hope, and charity, I may make a big noise and get a lot of people down the aisles, yet I am not apt to impart much of the Christian spirit or create much of a sense of the truly great happening of Christ.

The important thing in creative Christian witness is for the Christian to be himself as he witnesses for Christ. Of course, we can learn from others, which indeed we should. We can learn how to listen, what to say, when to press for a decision, yet witness by imitation is never wholly genuine. One must find his own way of witness and follow that way as his special vocation for Christ. One reason so many people shy away from witness is that they cannot feel comfortable following the other fellow's method. They have wrongly equated witness with a particular set of questions and an established formula of actions. For everyone to ask the same questions in the same way would not be creative witness. We need to see that the Christian life is much too rich, and its expressions too varied, for all of us to bear our Christian testimony in the same way. The secret is for the Christian to find his own unique calling.

When Paul said, "Be not conformed to this world: but be ye transformed" (Rom. 12:2), he was speaking of a great transaction of liberation. He was calling for man's uniqueness in Christ. This is not uniqueness as the world sees uniqueness, wherein to be different one must wear a beard or sideburns, go without shoes and socks, refuse to wear ties, and dress in odd, bizarre clothing and wear moon-sized glasses with amber lenses. One does not need to be strange to be unique. The uniqueness in Christ is transcendent in nature, and works much like Christian freedom works. The Christian may never be free *from* labor, but he can be free *in* his labor. In Christ he is free indeed. In the same way the Christian will never be unique in the sense of having three eyes instead of two; he will not be a clown among scholars, or a donkey among kings. His Christian uniqueness comes as he rises above the inevitable banalities of life and is released from his world-bound self and is unique indeed. True creative Christian witness is to give expression of his own Christ-conscious uniqueness.

Many Christians behave as though personal circumstances had meanings within themselves. For example, a man lets his job determine his attitude. He doesn't like it, so he sours. What he is doing, of course, is clothing his job with the fear, frustration, and doubt of his own soul. This man needs renewal. He needs to see that the moment he truly has "moral newness of soul" the old is replaced with the new. Faith, hope, love become the clothing of his life. Not only is he transformed, his job also is transformed. This experience of transformation is the experience of faith. It is that magic moment in life when one realizes that his milieu is not death, but eternal life. It is the realization that death is not his destiny. There is no possible way for one to know this except in Jesus Christ. Knowing him is the most creative experience of life, and sharing him is to creatively build the kingdom of God on earth.

Creative Christian witness makes the most of every personal contact. The most creative thing we can do is to become aware that every human contact bears witness for or against Christ. For the Christian there is no such thing as the unimportant conversation or the meaningless handshake. Creative Christian witness is eminently personal. The less personal it is, the less creative. In recent years our critics have often told us that we cheapen and nullify our evangelism. Some have said that we have tried to confine it to a formula. They accuse us of holding that there is no evangelism except in a protracted meeting.

Others say we have isolated the conversion experience into a series of steps to be taken without reference to the necessity for life change, and others that we have depended on gadgets such as ads in newspapers and pamphlets as though the gadgets themselves were the evangelistic witness. The most devastating critics say that we have failed to present the whole gospel for the whole man, allowing converts to see only a small portion of the matchless wonders of God in Christ. They also say that we have taken a mechanistic view of salvation, believing that if we did certain things then certain other things would eventually happen. Other critics say that the salvation experience itself has become mechanical, involving a few formalities and little of the great personal transactions of the New Testament.

I would say that if these critics are right, the time has come for a more creative evangelism. They perhaps are saying two things: One is that our present-day witness is largely mechanical or impersonal, and the other that we have failed to show the world that the Christian life is not something to be tacked onto a series of other life-determining events. For the Christian, being a Christian is the whole of life, and in the Christian enterprise the personal element in witness is absolutely fundamental.

American evangelism has its roots deep in the two great awakenings.[1] The first one started in 1726 when two young ministers in New Jersey began preaching a personal-experience Christianity: Gilbert Tennant, a Presbyterian, and Frelinghuysen, a Dutch Reformed. They were soon joined by Jonathan Edwards and George Whitefield. The impulse of this awakening lasted almost until the American Revolution. The heart of the Great Awakening was personal life-changing encounter with Christ. People were changed, and in changing they caught fire that they could easily pass to others. The mechanics of the awakening were protracted meetings, home fellowships, and the open-air service.

The second Great Awakening began around 1800, spontaneously in many different areas, especially in the South. Awakenings took place in Kentucky 1800–3, Tennessee 1800–12, Georgia 1827, and in many other areas. These continued through most of the century and their effects are still strongly felt even into this day. Again the personal was the dominant element. The modern concept of Christians as soul-winners came from these revivals. In the early years these soul-winners were not people who argued or whined for the faith but charismatic people who counseled seekers. The mechanics of the revival were the long-term summer revival, the camp meeting, grove services, and extensively organized evangelistic campaigns.

Some things need to be noted about these awakenings:

1. They took place among an immigrating people. Shubal Stearns, for example, a stalwart New England convert of the first Great Awakening, moved with a great number of other New Englanders from Massachusetts to North Carolina and

became a giant Christian leader and founder of churches. The whole country was on the move. People were open to new ideas and ready for new decisions. The era of the second Great Awakening saw America in the period of its greatest geographical expansion.

2. The new nation was in ferment. The period of the first awakening was also the period of all the forces that produced America's drive for independence. The second was the period that finally precipitated the Civil War. Most of our country's great political and social concepts were born during these periods.

3. The revivals were interdenominational in character. They reflected God moving more in the people than in the churches. It is true that they greatly strengthened and multiplied the denominations, yet God's Spirit seemed to be moving transcendent to the denominations.

4. The revivals were spontaneous. There were leaders, of course, and these leaders followed patterns of performance, but revival seemed to come regardless of what the leaders did. And frequently where there were no leaders. From historical perspective, the revivals do not appear to have been contrived.

5. The revivals operated almost wholly in the rural and frontier context. They were frequently most vigorous in the open country and isolated communities. Frequently when towns would spring up, the church would be a rural church a mile or two away in the open country. In great industrial cities like New York and Philadelphia the people were increasingly less sensitive to revival. Congregations in these cities would receive most of their members when rural folk moved to town.

6. The revivals brought a stricter discipline into the churches. People with a unique Christian experience were expected to live a different kind of Christian life. In the first awakening two terms developed: "new light" and "old light." The new light churches were those that wholly followed conversionist ideas of religious experience. The conversion experience was the initia-

tory rite, and marked the beginning of the separated life. The congregation considered itself responsible for the care of the individual Christian. Even the old lights who did not follow the conversionist ideas began to exercise a stricter discipline in their churches.

Even Christians forget about those revivals and what made them great. One common error is a feverish haste to perpetuate the mechanics of revival without the vital personal element. Another is the insistence that Christ always comes to man precisely in the same way in one generation as in another. We fail to see that the Holy Spirit knows more than one path into the soul of a man, and refuse to adapt our witness to new methods in the new times.

In this discussion I have tried to say that creative Christian witness can be one of two things: gadgetry or charisma. Gadgetry without charisma is worthless; but if one has charisma, gadgetry is not important; so always strive for charisma.

NOTES

1. See *History of the Baptists,* Robert G. Torbet, and encyclopedia articles on the Great Awakenings.

CHAPTER 4

Creative Learning

■ ■ ■

When one of my sons was about five years old, we moved into a new house. Eagerly he went exploring. He found the big trees with the swings just his size, a sandbox next to the garage, a long concrete driveway for his tricycle, a little hill on which to play, and a broad front porch just right for looking at a whole new world. After inspecting all of these new things, he came to his mother and said: "Mamma, is all of this really ours?" True Christian learning is a mind-stretching and spirit-building experience that brings us face to face with God's matchless love in Christ, with his forgiveness and his providence, with promise of power for daily living, with the assurance of eternal life. One by one we explore these great riches and realizing their meaning, we say: "Are these really ours?" Creative Christian learning makes the most out of the gifts of life and increases appreciation for them as life lengthens.

The true Christian life is experience, but not a dead mechanistic surface experience. It is a dynamic learning experience. This means that it moves forward and upward, and that it changes always in the direction of perfection. It means new discoveries and new insights. It is individuation of the highest kind, leading the person from one new life insight to another.

Sometimes a dreamer feels that he is light enough to fly and that he is present in an event about which he is dreaming, yet above it. Other times he feels that he is transported lightly from one event to another, always part of these events, yet detached from them. The learning Christian is like this. He participates in the life of this world, yet his special experience with Christ makes him transcendental to it. It is this quality of special understanding that marks him as different and gives him a special kind of joy.

No responsible Christian would ignore the basic truth on which his faith is built. The facts are that God has moved toward man through Christ his Son, that the Son did live as God on earth, that he died on the cross as the ultimate experience of God's love and became the atoning link between God and man, that he was raised from the grave, that he is at God's right hand, and that someday he will return again. These elemental Christian facts are the basis of our faith. They constitute also a value system in which God himself understood as love is the highest value.

Of course, there are many more Christian facts, as we surely know from our study of the New Testament; and there are many more values, all of which are sustained by this incomparable concept of God as love. In Panama there is an old church built early in the sixteenth century, almost one hundred years before Plymouth in New England. The guides proudly show the tourist a great stone arch in which there is no mortar. The special point they make is that it has stood through countless earthquakes and hurricanes, while all about it are other buildings in ruin. The guide says: "Look at the keystone, that is the secret." The keystone of the Christian value system is the love of God, and its manifestation is his Son dying on a cross.

Yet we miss the point in creative Christian learning if we see God's love only as an idea and if we fail to meet his love in face-to-face personal confrontation. We have not learned our first lesson in creative Christianity if God has not broken outside the rigid boundaries of an idea and become a living person.

Meister Eckhart, the great German mystic, put it as only a mystic can: "There is an agent in my soul which is perfectly sensitive to God. I am sure of this as I am that I am alive: nothing is as near me as God is. God is nearer to me than I am to myself. My being depends on God's intimate presence. So, too, he is near to a stick or a stone but they do not know it. If the stick knew God and recognized how near he is, as the holy angels know such things, the stick would be as blessed as the angels." [1] Very few of us are mystics; nevertheless it is possible somewhere somehow for every person to be sensitive to God as a loving living being. Jesus Christ assured this. He bridged the greatest of all generation gaps, that which separated man and God, and made it possible for man to feel God and to know him as a loving Father. I became aware of this long ago when as a child I use to sit between the cotton bales of the cotton yard, and looking up at the blue sky by day and the stars by night, I would pray simply: "God, thy will be done." He came to me as a persistent presence, as an experience that has grown more wondrous as the years passed. He emerged from being an idea in a Sunday School book to becoming a constant companion in whose spell I've always been held, even when I've tried to escape. It was God as confrontation in Christ that turned me from a dead stick to an eternal soul.

But creative Christian learning does not stop with this initial transforming experience or with this divine-human encounter. It goes on to many encounters with many people, all of them controlled by that initial encounter with God. Just as a man says either yes or no to God, he says yes or no to people. A no to God usually means a no to life and a no to people. I've often wondered which would happen if early in the morning I put a tiny, tiny sign on the front door of my office building that said a simple "no," and inside a slightly larger one. After that several signs each larger saying "no" until on my office door that was a no three feet tall, and inside one ten feet tall. What would people feel by the time they sat at my desk overshadowed by that big black no? What would happen if I replaced all of these signs with yes? Would the mood be different?

Yes, I think it would be different. That tiny little "no" at the front door means a shouting "no" wherever I work and live. Our little "no" to God means a great "no" to life and to people. Moreover, the little "no's" of our lives have ways of growing. Creative Christian learning starts with a little "yes" to God. The further we move toward the end of life the bigger that "yes" becomes. If I really have said "yes," and mean what I said, then people will come looking for me. They will feel uplifted by my presence. They will know I have found the secret of successful living.

I am not really learning as a Christian until by my spirit I teach others. It is important for me to bear witness to the facts of the gospel, but it is doubly important that I bear witness by my spirit. Other people hear the gospel more from my spirit than from my preaching. It is by the Spirit of Christ within me that I am able to communicate with other persons and influence them for good. A poor father was ill on Christmas, mostly because of personal frustrations he had not been able to handle. In the great joy of opening toys his eight-year-old son shouted with laughter. The father asked the boy to be quiet. Later in the day the father was upset when the boy could not put together a complicated toy. By nighttime the spirit of the child was crushed and the father was in misery. It was the beginning of the decay of communications which have never been restored. The poor father has repented a thousand times, and the son has forgotten; yet the scars are still present.

The father is a reverse example of God. He moved against his son, God moves toward us. He acted selfishly, God acted in love. He broke off communications with a harsh word; God established communication with his eternal Word. The father is powerless within himself to bridge the gap; God laid his own life across the gap. There is one hope for that poor father. It is that he can learn the spirit of Christ, and approach his son, not as himself, but as Christ in him. Whatever God is doing in his approach to man in Christ, he will continue to do through the father as the father approaches the son. The poor father had better not get the foolish idea that he might die for the son, as Christ died for him. In this he would be playing God and taking to himself responsibility for atonement. It would be to try to duplicate the work of Christ. Creative Christian learning brings us along in our Christian experience to our teaching of others not from what we are, but from what Christ is in us. Presuming to teach the Christian life from any other pose is egotistical ineptitude, and contempt for Almighty God's plan for the ages.

Learning is creative if it finds its basic lessons in the words of God. People who do not accept the wisdom and the authority of the Bible are in no position for Christian growth. They have no solid basis on which to build a spiritual life. This claim for the Bible can be seen in several different ways. Some will look upon it as a defense of the Bible as a talisman, as a book that produces magic results.

Others will see this challenge as defense of what they call "narrow biblicism." The critics of Christ and his church usually get around to this point on the grounds that they have a higher understanding of the Bible. They are more interested in saying what it is not, than what it is. I am well aware of the apparent overlappings and alleged contradictions of the Bible, but I am also aware of the integrity and authority of the Bible. I do not take it for what it says in one verse, but in all verses. The book of Job is a dramatic example of what the whole Bible means to me. From it I could proof text some pretty drastic accusations against God. I could take the speeches of Elihu and other critics of Job and prove him wrong and them right. But I refuse to look at Job except as a whole, so I see unfolding before me a book that has double authority, the authority of God's revelation and the authority of proven human wisdom. Job is the oldest book in the Bible, perhaps the oldest in the world. The twentieth-century critics who say, "Ho hum, just another book among all that has ever been written," do not frighten me at all.

The true Christian learner sees the Bible as the testimony of the ages, as God's way of speaking to man in terms of his own experience, as eternity leaning forward into time, as God's cooperation with man to help him discover faith, hope, and love. The true learning Christian does not take the words of God arbitrarily or rotely, but as ideas to be rubbed against each other for the fire they will reveal. Nor does he take them carelessly, dismissing as untrue what he does not understand, or discarding as unbelievable what is not logical to him.

Suppose, for example, man scissors Genesis out of the Bible. What then is his explanation for the beginning of the community of God? Indeed how does he explain first causes? Let him scissor it out as untrue; if he is honest he will come back to it, believing it more than ever, not as a narration but as truth. Let him with those same scissors cut out hell from the Bible, then let him paste back in his answer to questions like: What happens to man's free will when he is not given an ultimate choice? Or how is evil to be punished? If he goes frantically on trying to make his own scripture, his little pieces of paper will grow so many and so complicated that he will be searching for a summary and when he finds it he will look at his scissors and say: "You betrayed me. The answers were there in the Bible all the time."

Others will see in my appeal for the Bible a book for creative Christian learning and a call to understand it as words fitly spoken like "apples of gold in pictures of silver" (Prov. 25:11), but not as a flat-colored drawing. The Bible is no mere art masterpiece to be hung in the treasure of the heart. It is a carving in full relief. It has depth and perspective. It has weight and substance. It can be seen from all sides and it can be handled and understood. Moreover, it is a masterpiece of highest value. The words of God are gold, gold that nourishes, and they are silver, silver that strengthens. They are the words of life to be rightly handled. They are the foundation of our lives, on which if we build, we will endure the wind, the rains, and the floods. The words of God are to be believed, yes; but far more, they are to be lived. It is in the living that we discover their truth and their eternity.

Learning is creative if it moves from the words of God to the Word of God. Unless our learning moves from the words of God to the Word of God, then we have not had the one truly creative experience that gives us eternal life and makes us citizens of heaven. The Bible looks always in one direction, toward Jesus Christ.

John makes this very clear in his mighty hymn to the Word in which he said: "In the beginning was the Word, and the Word was with God, and the Word was God. He was in the beginning with God; all things were made through him, and without him was not anything made that was made. In him was life, and the life was the light of men. The light shines in the darkness, and the darkness has not overcome it" (John 1:1–5, RSV).

In primeval time when God laid the foundations of the world and breathed into the dust of the earth his own life, and gave that dust his own image, the creature he made was enough like him to see his visions and to think his thoughts. Gifted men, closest to God, and most touched by his Spirit caught the great vision. They heard the words of his voice and they saw that God was always moving toward man, attempting to speak to him the Word of Love. The Old Testament is the record of spiritual geniuses who kept hearing these words. Their insight led them to realize that the words of God would someday be understood as the Word of God.

These geniuses wrote down what they heard and saw, and though they did not themselves always fully understand the full meaning of their visions, they did consciously share in God's great effort to close the gap between himself and man. David, one of them, cried out: "Thou didst speak in a vision to thy faithful one" (Ps. 89:19, RSV). The sense of these visions was "that all the people of the earth may know that the Lord is God, there is none else" (1 Kings 8:60). The eternity of the vision was undoubted, "The grass withereth, the flower fadeth, but the word of God shall stand forever" (Isa. 40:8). To these geniuses the word was imperishable and alive forever.

They understood well the personal side of God's speaking to man. They spoke of the Servant, the Son, the Chosen One, the Branch, the Holy One, and the Messiah. Mostly they saw the unfolding word as the Servant. This daring concept had to be a self-revelation of God, for no man holding an idea of God, could ever create out of his own limited mind a vision of God with attributes that seem less than God.

They saw him as the mighty servant who "will bring forth justice to the nations" (Isa. 42:1, RSV). Who would be "a light to the nations" (42:6), and who would "startle many nations" (52:15). But they saw him also as the suffering servant, as one who "hath borne our griefs, and carried our sorrows . . . stricken, smitten of God, and afflicted" (Isa. 53:4) and "numbered with the transgressors; and he bare the sin of many, and made intercession for the transgressors" (Isa. 53:12).

But he was not merely a servant of deeds, he also was a servant of "loving-kindness" the one whose mercy endureth forever. The Hebrew word used to describe a person of this special quality is *hhasidh*. Willis J. Beecher said, that when *hhasidh* is applied to God, "he is presented as the person in whom his own lovingkindness dwells, whence it may be manifested for the benefit of his creatures." [2] God is always moving toward man to deposit all of his love in man. He does this through the suffering servant of lovingkindness, Jesus Christ who as the *hhasidh* speaks to us *because he is the hhasidh*. He is the word of love, God's final word to man. When God spoke through him he saw all there was of himself to say.

This does not mean that we understand all that was said, or could ever understand it. It does mean that if we really want to hear the words of God we must hear them through his Word of Love, through Jesus Christ, for in him is life and his life is the light of men.

As you have read these words you have probably gotten lost in the rhetoric. This is almost always true when we deal with abstract ideas. Certain modern poets have no meaning for me because I don't know what they are talking about. It is as simple as this: I don't know what they are talking about because I don't know what they are talking about. This does not mean these poets have nothing to say. It does mean I don't know what they are saying because I don't know what their words mean. If I want to know what they are saying I must learn their words.

It is the same thing with God's great spiritual truth. I must not expect to know it without learning and so I must learn the words of God. Moreover, I must not expect to know without being taught, and it is in the words of God where God himself becomes my teacher. If I search his words and submit to his leadership, then soon a miracle will happen, the miracle of creative learning, the miracle of understanding—and the focus of that understanding is the Word.

Suddenly we are back in the rhetoric. How can the focus of our personal understanding on God be the Word? Imagine you and me together in conversation. It is a warm spring day and we are sitting in the shade of a maple tree. We see the robins in the tall grass, the iris blooming in the garden, and squirrels scampering about the lawn. Suddenly all of this recedes into the background as we talk to each other. I am trying to understand you, and you are trying to understand me. The things that exchange between us are words. They are the reflections of our inner selves. They are sounds and inflections, but they also are heart and soul. They are meaning. They are life. If I am man, and you are woman and in this idyllic setting I say, "I love you," then you see and feel something you never experienced before. You hear my word as me. It becomes alive to you, and you take it as promise. The spoken word suddenly has become personality and experience. Suppose I offer marriage, then the promise of a family has become a manifestation of that word of love. The children will come to exist not merely because they exist, but because of the word of love. They exist because love existed from the beginning.

It is something like this between you and God. From before the foundation of the world it has been his purpose to engage you in conversation. But he faces a problem; it is much easier for two human beings to talk together under a maple tree than for you and him to talk together across the centuries. So what does God do? He broods, he thinks, he dreams, and out of his nature of love he enters into a dialogue with all men, slowly and painfully, in terms of their own understanding and experience; hence, we have the law and the prophets of the Old Testament. He shouts, he thunders, he walks quietly in the cold of the day, he comes as a still small voice in a cave, or the holy, holy, holy high and lifted up in the temple. He uses a thousand ways to get attention, and always it is the word of God at work. "And God *said,* Let there be light" (Gen. 1:3). "And God *said,* Let us make man in *our* image" (Gen. 1:26). "Through faith we understand that the worlds were framed by the word of God" (Heb. 11:3). "He sent his word" (Ps. 107: 20). "For the Lord *spoke* thus to me" (Isa. 8:11). The speaking is always personal and always creative.

Finally, when the time was right, God showed the world something it had never seen before. It is set forth in the opening verses of John's Gospel. Martin Luther called these words "the one, tender, real crown jewel-Gospel of them all," Lenski said they were "the central jewel set in pure gold." What God wanted us to see was that just as a man spoke words: "I love you" becomes the irrevocable expression of the nature and commitment of his life, Jesus Christ, the Word, the *logos,* the servant, the *hhasidh,* the lovingkindness of himself, becomes the finally irrevocable and forever sealed word of himself.

Learning is creative if experience of the Word of God renews life. A young man trains for nine years to become a history professor. Suddenly, as if in a dream, he realizes the world has misled him. Instead of being one Ph.D. with the choice of a dozen jobs, he is one of scores of Ph.D.'s in history desperately fighting for one of a few available jobs. The telephone doesn't ring, the postman doesn't call, no friend knocks; anger, frustration, emptiness, despair, grief. He develops a serious skin disease and stomach ulcers.

A young woman dreams of a home and a family, and faithfully prepared herself to be a housewife and mother. Graduation from college—no proposal. She takes a job for which she is not prepared, in which she does moderately well, but finds no happiness. Still no proposal. Life becomes a dark cloud. She broods over her disappointment and gets twinges in her side. Her digestive system loses its rhythym and life is miserable. To this young woman, the twinges are physical, but to her doctor they are her broken dreams.

The world has a curious theory about her hunger and the young teacher's ulcers. It says: "Get married and the twinges will vanish, or get a job teaching history, and the ulcers will go away." That sounds plausible, and may work for a time. Yet again and again, you have seen it, the old trouble returns when the pressures mount. The girl marries and her symptoms disappear, but they come again when her husband fails in his job. The man finds a professorship, but his ulcers flair up when someone else is promoted ahead of him.

These two examples could be multiplied scores of times out of your experience. Learning to cope with our problems is one of the basic challenges of life. There are a few people who seem to be able to do it out of their own strength. However, most of us must have help from outside ourselves. We simply cannot find inside ourselves the power to meet the problems of life. Sometimes it seems, the older we get the more difficult it is to find solutions. We are driven to our own special Gethsemanes and the ultimate confession of absolute helplessness. Life gets tired and runs down, and like a toy balloon the morning after the party, for all its evening brightness and gaiety, it rests in the dust, flabbily and half empty, a wrinkled inert shadow of its former glory. The human soul has a way of threatening to collapse before its enemies. There may have been no sin in the young woman or young man's life, except the sin of pride and the sin of the lack of faith, but these sins are enough to paralyze and destroy and they are the sins at the root of all other sins.

What these two people needed was renewal, not the superficial renewal of the Fourth of July spent in the mountains, or Labor Day at the beach, but renewal of the soul and spirit that comes from being in touch with the source of all life, the renewal of God's Spirit at work in life.

The sacrament of this renewal is the Word. Suppose the young man heard from a college dean the word, "I want you as a professor," or the young woman from her sweetheart the word, "I want you as my wife," there would have come renewal of a kind. The sincere word bridges the gap between human beings and restores vitality and confidence. There is nothing so healing as the rightly spoken word. Between a father and a son, it is the word of confidence; between a husband and a wife the word of trust; between two friends, the word of admiration; between employer and employee, the word of reliability; between enemies, the word of respect. Rightly spoken, the word heals and strengthens, it enlightens and elevates.

Between God and man the Word is the Word, and his name is Love. He is Jesus Christ. God has been speaking it from before the foundation of the world. The Word heals, the Word strengthens, the Word enlightens, the Word elevates, and the Word makes all things new. God's Word to man is his unqaulified "yes" to man. It is the speaking of his own heart, the cry of his own nature, the utterance of his eternity. Hearing that Word is renewal. When we begin to hear, it is not the end of something, but beginning. "He that is of God heareth God's words" (John 8:47). Any ordinary word spoken, unless heard in relationship to the Word of God, is meaningless. Whether a word has meaning or not, is true or not, is real or not, depends solely on how that word is related to God. Without God, no word spoken has any meaning.

No wonder Jesus Christ himself said: "I make all things new" (Rev. 21:5), or that he said: "This is my blood of the new testament" (Mark 14:24). His entrance into the experiences of man is the truly great creative miracle of the ages. In him all things do indeed become new. "If any man be in Christ, he is a new creature: old things are passed away; behold, all things are become new" (2 Cor. 5:17). "Be renewed in the spirit of your mind; and that ye put on the new man" (Eph. 4: 23–24).

So God comes to us in the Word and we are never again the same.

NOTES

1. Raymond Bernard Blakney, translator, *Meister Eckhart* (New York: Harper & Brothers Publishers, 1941) p. 129.

2. Willis J. Beecher, *The Prophets and the Promise* (Oklahoma City: Semco Color Press) p. 314.

CHAPTER 5

Creative Service

■ ■ ■

What is Christian service?

Priscilla is certain she knows. Five times a week she goes to church. Her special dedication is Bible study. She never keeps a book unless it is filled with references to the Bible, and one afternoon each week she attends a special Bible class for women. Priscilla is a good woman with a wholesome attitude and excellent personal habits, but there is little else the pastor can get her to do. Priscilla has underscored in her Bible words which she says are the motto of her life.

Enoch is just as certain he knows the full meaning of Christian service. He is faithful to church and supports most of its activities. His hobby is rock hunting to which he devotes many of his Saturdays and his vacations. He is also a skilled mechanic and operates his own scales repair business. The nature of his hobby and his work require him to spend many hours alone which he says gives him opportunity for prayer. There is no question about Enoch's basic Christian goodness. He tithes his income, attends the meetings of the church, and studies his Sunday School lesson. Visitors who see Enoch at church comment on the joy and serenity of his countenance. Many think of him as a saint. "A Christian," he would say, "is one who puts his faith in the Lord and lives as good as he can. He lets his light shine that God may be glorified."

Martha is all for the church and its services, but she is constantly talking about how the church must go out into the world and do things. She took two delinquent girls into her home and organized a child care center for working mothers. She regularly visits the home for unwed mothers, and she teaches a Sunday School class at the girls' reformatory. Despite her many good works and faithfulness to the church, not many think of her as a saint. In fact, they observe that at times she seems edgy and harassed. Secretly she clings to some words of reassurance from Jesus.

Peter is Martha's husband, but his idea of Christian service is quite different. He is patient with her good works though at times he wonders about the drain on her physical and emotional strength. He thinks she overlooks the point of Christian service, which he believes is soul-winning. Peter never misses an opportunity to speak up for the Lord, and spends many of his evenings talking to people about becoming Christians. He has organized some of the men of his church to help him in his evangelism. His pastor frankly says that without Peter the church would lose members. Peter denies this, for basically he is a humble self-effacing man. Nobody thinks of him as a saint, and he is frequently left off church committees. When pressed for an explanation of his witness, he says: "God calls some to be leaders, but he has called me to serve."

Peter has a brother named Matt, a well-educated man who knows his way about in the community. While Peter is in someone's home talking about being a Christian and Martha is counseling delinquent girls, Matt is meeting with the city's crime commission in effort to do something about dope traffic. The pastor says that he is one of the best committee members in the church, but that he will not take a regular job teaching a class on ushering. Matt wants to be free to respond to the community's crisis needs, which he does not merely as a businessman, but as a concerned Christian citizen. Secretly he says to himself, Jesus asked us to let our light shine in the community. That's what I am doing.

Now imagine these five people in conversation with the pastor. Priscilla quite emphatically says: "What the church needs is to quit doing so many foolish things and study the Bible. That is what it means to perform Christian service."

"No," says Martha, "genuine Christian service is ministry and mission actions. We aren't going to prove ourselves without it."

"You are both wrong," says Peter. "God meant for all of us to be soul-winners."

"I surely would hate to be as narrow as you people," said Matt. "Until we take our places in the power centers of the community we aren't going to win the world to Christ."

"All of you are wrong," said Enoch. "The best evidence of a Christian is the Christian spirit. We are the ones in whom the mind and character of Christ should be daily evident."

The pastor, a very able man, and alert to the need for many different kinds of Christian expressions said: "No, Enoch, you are not all wrong, but you are all right. Christian service is not one thing but many things. No two people can live the Christian life in the same way. I happen to know that each one of you lives by some very special words of our Lord: 'Let your light so shine before men, that they may see your good works and give glory to your Father who is in heaven' (Matt. 5:16, RSV). You are all right in this, for that saying covers many different kinds of service."

God gives each person his own unique Christian service vocation. Church members who carefully read the Bible are surely impressed with the variety of talents and services of the great servants of God. Moses knew the law and could lead people, but diplomacy and speechmaking were not his talents. To get the most out of Moses, God had to send along his brother Aaron to help him; yet Aaron by himself was almost worthless.

Amos and Isaiah both worked in the same big league of prophecy, yet they were two different men with opposite backgrounds and approaches. Isaiah was the sophisticated city man, whose knowledge of the world, sensitive spiritual vision and fierce diplomacy kept him in the courts of kings almost all of his life. From Isaiah's writings one can visualize a mental and spiritual giant with burning eyes and soft hands. Amos perhaps was a grubby sheep farmer with calloused hands and shaggy head. He lacked Isaiah's diplomacy and elegance, but he brought a compelling spirit to everything he said. His words were rough and to the point. These two prophets would have had difficulty identifying with each other, but they were each essential to God's work.

The same kind of contrast separated Peter and Paul. Peter was a violent impulsive man who lived with his feelings close to the surface. He would act first and then think. He would never understand why Paul took three years in the wilderness to think over his experience on the Damascus road. Peter was a man whose epitaph might have been "Born Ready." He was a man of action, and had you asked him about his philosophy, he might have asked you what you meant.

In contrast Paul was a born thinker who carefully weighed his words and who found prison a satisfying place for working out some of his most profound ideas. He was the philosopher who loved deliberative meetings and who advanced ideas that were far beyond Peter's simple concepts, so much so that Peter said they were hard to understand and rebelled against them. If both Paul and Peter were transported into one of our church conventions of the twentieth century, they would stand on opposite sides of the same question. It is likely that Peter would stand with the masses, and Paul with the leaders; yet both were ordained of God and essential to the work of God on earth. They illustrate clearly variety among the servants of God.

Paul acknowledged this variety. He said: "There are varieties of gifts . . . varieties of service . . . varieties of working, but it is the same God who inspires them all in every one. To each is given the manifestation of the Spirit for the common good" (1 Cor. 12:4–7, RSV). Paul in these strong words is stressing the unity of the church, a unity that is in God, not in man, and a unity that frankly admits the lack of uniformity among the members. Not only is this lack of uniformity a clear reflection of human differences, it is a plain proof of human freedom. God makes men different because he made them free.

In my early days as pastor, I was constantly fretting because church members would not always do what I thought they ought to do. Sue Hillin could play the violin and she was expert with children, but she would have nothing to do with the young women's missionary activities and this annoyed me. Billy Jo Braggs kept our little library in perfect order and was a good Sunday School teacher, but she would have nothing to do with church training. Fred Parsons gave me wonderful advice on working with people, but he would not be a deacon. I was not content with what the people did, and was constantly disturbed by what they did not do. The harder I pushed, the more they resisted. It took years for me to learn that in the Christian community, the differences in gifts and service of the members is directly related to their personal freedom, and that God himself is responsible both for their interests and their freedom. It was a great day for me when I learned that the congregation would not fall to pieces even if everybody did not do everything. I learned finally that the variety is one of the secrets of a dynamic church.

God gives each person his own unique nature, and one cannot serve the Lord unless he acts consistent with that nature. Man's work for God is bound up with the manner of person that he is. His freedom is to act in keeping with uniqueness. He becomes false when he acts in keeping with the manner and uniqueness of others. He must be himself, else God has no use for him.

God speaks to us in terms of our uniqueness. He recognizes the divided nature of man, and calls man in order to help him escape the false selves that mutilate and destroy personality and usefulness. Surely God must smile, when he hears one of our popular singers, such as Frank Sinatra, singing "I gotta be me." He would say: "Okay, Frank, which me? The good me or bad me? The brave me or coward me? The loving me or hating me?"

The real struggle God has with man is getting him to face the authentic "me," the one marked for immortality. He knows that history is strewn with the heartache of men who went off after the wrong "me." Yes, he calls out to man, and he who hears this call has an awesome problem.

Jonah is one of the best examples of a person who struggled to find himself. His true calling lay in Nineveh though he thought it lay in Tarshish. Following the wrong "me" he bought a ticket to Tarshish and stepped on the ship a divided man. A storm came, and Jonah knew that it was the voice of God; he told the sailors they were doomed because he was doomed. "Cast me forth into the sea; so shall the sea be calm unto you" (Jonah 1:12). From inside the belly of the big fish Jonah called to the Lord: "I am cast out of thy sight; yet I will look again toward thy holy temple" (2:4). Finally God brought him to Nineveh and he preached for the people to repent or perish. Much to Jonah's surprise they repented but because he was still divided he prayed: "It is better for me to die than to live" (4:3). He built a tent and prepared to die. God grew a gourd vine to shade him, and then cut it down with a worm. It took all this for Jonah to see that God had a uniqueness for him and that surrendering to this uniqueness was his only way to wholeness. God was calling Jonah through the changing events of his life. Once he dared to tie himself to that call, its power in his life was inevitable.

Mary, Priscilla, Enoch, Peter, and Matt are five different people performing five kinds of services. They have definite Christian convictions, and they do the things they like to do in service to God. Their service fits their temperaments and their abilities. While their choices of service are basic in God's work, they do not exhaust the possibilities for Christian vocation.

God expects our Christian service to be performed in keeping with the purpose and the needs of the body of Christ. Like it or not, whether it seems true or not, whether we can understand it or not, the truth always remains, that Christian service is not possible apart from the worker's identity with the body of Christ; the Christian cause is a community affair. It is not one person performing churchly tasks, but all the members at work in ways that complement each other. The apostle Paul's picture of the body having many members and all the members appropriately working together is not merely an example of Christian service; it is the essence of Christian service.

In God's service, the little deeds do not merely complement the big ones, or the big deeds, the little ones. Some people seem to think that what the meek do is merely to help the powerful accomplish the work, or for the powerful to help the meek. Eugene Stockwell, a missionary to Uruguay, tells of a poor member of the church who came to an evening service with a cookie tin under his arm. The man dropped in a few pennies and said it is for a building for the church, which then had no meeting place of its own. Four years later, a wealthy woman added $20,000 to the growing contents of that cookie tin, and the church was built. The point is not that the man started it, or the woman finished it, but that both were performing their service to God. As long as Matt, the Christian who chooses to serve in the public arena, remembers his place as a member of the body of Christ, his work will have true Christian significance, but if he ever attempts to function without this awareness, he becomes something less than a Christian in performing his service.

Imagine the five people, Mary, Priscilla, Enoch, Peter, and Matt, meeting in a committee to develop a true church program. How would they go about developing a report? One method, of course, would be in terms of goals that should be met. There is nothing wrong with setting church goals, except too often they are either mere figures which lack life or meaning and are hard to measure. The most ideal goals have a way of becoming stale and lifeless unless there is living power available to translate them into reality. The committee would find that the goals are needed, but that something else is needed even more.

The second method would stress the responsibility the church has to God and the world. Unless the members are careful, the committee will break down as each member tries to nudge the others into accepting his special version of where responsibility lies. "Worship and the devout life," says Enoch. "No," replies Peter, "soul-winning." Matt says: "Public service." Priscilla: "Good works." Mary: "Teaching the Bible." Wisely, the pastor calls them back to the realities of the New Testament. "All these things are our responsibilities," he says. But suppose the committee comes to the congregation with a set of goals and a set of general responsibilities. Is it likely there would be much response to their suggested plans for action? There would not be much creativity in that.

The third method would be to ask frankly and honestly, where is God at work in the world and how does he want us to join him in what he is doing? Creative Christian service keeps in mind the timeless Christian goals and it stresses all forms of personal service, but most of all, it goes where the action is, and takes its place as a servant to whatever cause is being served. The service agenda of the church should be in keeping with what God is doing here and now in our own day and time. The Christian surely must believe the words of Jesus: "My Father is working still, and I am working" (John 5:17, RSV). Whatever the committee would recommend in answer to the basic questions on religious tasks, appropriate actions and valid effects, it must recommend in terms of dialogue with the world.

The members of this committee should emerge from their work as renewed Christians especially if they face God's reality in the world. Basically they would not have changed, and yet they would have changed. Mary would still teach the Bible, but not as speaking to the past; she would teach it as God's living dialogue having bearing on the problems of her own day and time. Priscilla would be less fretful, for she would realize that God works, Jesus works, and she also works. Enoch would see that there are differences between being good in a good community and good in a bad community, and that whatever sainthood he has must be manifest to the unchristian as well as to the Christian. Peter would be more effective in soul-winning, for he would realize that God is more at work than he is. Matt would go into the power centers realizing that not all the power he was contending with belongs to the world; indeed some of it belonged to God. Approaching their own special tasks as a part of the total task would give them a new sense of the vitality and the mobility of the church. It would renew the experiences of church in their own lives, and it would do much to break up the criticism that so many people make against the church. Moving into those areas where God's action is taking place, they would have a greater sense of living meaningfully in their own age.

Christian service begins in whatever place and circumstance the Christian finds himself. Some pleaders for Christian ministry talk constantly about service in jails, ghettos, reformatories, halfway houses, and other similar institutions for the poor and the indigent. This is good, and too much emphasis cannot be placed on this kind of Christian service. The world needs more people willing to work in these areas, but to conceive of Christian ministry solely in terms of these unfortunate people is misunderstanding Christian service. It is to erect a service ideal that is impossible for all people to attain. Christian service was not invented just for the poor in the world's goods and the prisoners in steel and concrete jails. The parable on which much Christian social action is based means also that even the rich are poor, and the well are sick, and the free are in jail. It requires us to see that human need starts with our next door neighbor and in our own households. Priscilla would be surprised if she knew what is probably true, that her husband needs her personal Christian ministry about as much as the girls in the reformatory. He doesn't complain, but just the same he could use a few more better balanced meals, and a clean house at least once a week.

To expect everybody to go to the ghetto overlooks the fact that some people would be out of place in the ghettos. Take Billy Graham, for example. His calling is evangelism of the most traditional kind. He works at it day and night. There are those who might say Mr. Graham should stop and teach a Sunday School class in the reform school. This would be foolish. He is a public figure unable even to eat a meal in a restaurant without harassment. His strength is not what he does in the ghetto but in the White House or on the Tonight Show, preaching on television and in conversation with presidents and other public figures. His ministry starts not only with his calling and with his life style but also with his natural life setting. This broader concept of Christian ministry puts creative service in reach of every Christian every hour of the day. It does not depend on structures that transport people into scenes where they are unnatural intruders and have no instinctive empathy. Moreover, it puts upon every church the responsibility for serving its natural community not merely the community of geography, but also the community of interests.

God depends upon many different kinds of services for the progress of his work. By now you have guessed that Martha, Priscilla, Enoch, Peter, and Matt are inventions to help carry the points I wished to make about creative Christian service. Have you seen something else about them? Each represents one of the basic functions of a New Testament church. Enoch represents worship; Martha represents teaching; Priscilla, ministry; Peter, soul-winning; and Matt, application or involvement; and like many other people, they each think his special interest is the most important. What their pastor keeps saying to them is true. "All five are important, and all five are essential."

The point where I quarrel with involvement is where its advocates assume that involvement alone is the answer. Nobody can question Jesus' involvement with the world as an example to us. Did not God send forth his Son into the world? "God was in Christ, reconciling the world unto himself" (2 Cor. 5:19). To fail the world is to fail Jesus Christ; yet one must be very careful that involvement in affairs of the world does not cut off other vital Christian functions.

Ministry also is important. Ministry and involvement are alike in that both turn out to the world and both represent the church at work for others. Ministry is personal and centers in persons. Involvement or application is institutional and centers in ideas and movements. Minstry is more what one person does in service to others; involvement is what we are able to do through the power centers and social structures of the community.

The two sides of the unexpendable coin of poverty are uselessness and hopelessness. If the poor ever feel that there is work to do and something will come of it, they acquire a new self-respect and a new dignity. Their pockets may be empty as ever, but for them there is hope because their spirit has begun to live again.

T. S. Eliot in "Murder in the Cathedral" presents a picture of peril and poverty as disastrous as any to be seen in Chicago and Nashville. For seven torturous years the village of Canterbury has been disorganized and leaderless. The merchants cheat the people, laborers try to hide in the fields, drought burns up the crops and dries up the rivers, October comes without a harvest, and the women are forced to take refuge in the Cathedral that promises no safety. The community is without protection and the soldiers are coming to murder the archbishop.

The women sense the involvement of all mankind in the terrible deed, and in this great partnership of wrong they find their work. They sing:

> We are soiled by filth that we cannot clean united to super-
> natural vermin,

It is not we alone, it is not the house, it is not the city that is
defiled,
But the world that is wholly foul.

Clear the air! clean the sky! wash the wind! take the stone
from the stone, take the skin from the arm, take the muscle
from the bone, and wash them. Wash the stone, wash the
bone, wash the brain, wash the soul, wash them wash them! [1]

The work of the Christian is to wash the whole world, using
every kind of Christian service. It takes it all.

NOTES

1. T. S. Eliot, "Murder in the Cathedral," *Complete Poems and
Plays* (New York, Harcourt, Brace and Co.) p. 214.

CHAPTER 6

Creative Community

■ ■ ■

So your son is a hippy-type—or your grandson or your neighbor's son. His hair grows longer and longer, his dress is careless. He wears beads; he goes barefoot most of the time and he will not be trapped into responsibility. His adolescence is prolonged year after year, and you are in cultural shock. You are afraid he may be dabbling in narcotics. You grit your teeth and do your duty, you smile kindly, you talk as though nothing bothered you, and you kiss him good-by. You do all this, knowing that by the minute the gulf between you is growing wider and wider, and you ask over and over: Where will it all end?

In the night when you cannot sleep you count your questions like sheep. Where have I failed? What has come over him? Why does he do it? Is there anything I can do? What has gone wrong with the world? O Lord, why, why, why?

If you are a young parent and your children are "neatniks" you look at their short hair and their clean hands and ask: "Will it happen to us?" You look at your neighbor's grown-up children and ask: "What is wrong with us?"

Probably the most asked question of our day is: "What has gone wrong? Where have we failed?" There is more soul searching around these questions than there has been for a long time. All of society is in ferment, and all people who think seriously about life are trying to find answers. They truly want to know what is wrong, why it is wrong and what can be done about it.

The horror we feel is heightened when we realize that some youth are caught in a net which they tie tighter and tighter around themselves. In a national conference to discuss problems facing the churches, one young man was present whose long hair was tied with a ribbon at the neck. He wore beads as a girl would wear them and was dressed in a bizarre costume completely different from others. His special interest was violence, and in a voice that scarcely could be heard he would say: "We must use violence to stop all the terror in the world. It is the only way." He would plead for peace and criticize policemen for their violence. He seemed to be moved by some vision of terror to come and would place his hand on his head as though to try to pull from it a fuller understanding. He spoke as though he himself was a symbol of all the things that the world hates, and as though all its problems must be solved immediately without regard to the nature of new problems created. When speakers would analyze bad social situations, he would nod his head in strong agreement or disagreement. His crusading spirit was unmistakable. In another age he might have been a crusader on his way to the Holy Land, or a pioneer preacher in a brush arbor revival.

Two older men were trying to analyze his actions.

One asked: "Do you think he shows signs of paranoia?"

"Definitely," answered the older. "The paranoia of many of today's youth is their most notable characteristic. They are afraid and they are so self-conscious that they think the world is after them, and in a sense this is true, for we have pampered youth and have turned on them with a deep hatred. If they are paranoic, it is because we have made them that way. There are other reasons for this strangeness such as increased information, greater mobility, and the loss of community. Let's not be too hard on this young man because we have made him what he is."

This man was trying to answer the question. "What happened?"

His answers are interesting. First, *increased information*. To-day's youth are the first generation who cannot remember when there was no television. Nightly they have been subject to ex-pert analysis of what was wrong. Half their conscious lives they have had a steady diet of war and violence. Many feel as did a young taxi driver in Washington, D. C., when the radio told of more air raids over Cambodia. He suddenly switched it off and said: "Bombing, bombing, bombing, all I hear is death." The effect of unrestricted radio, TV, and other news media is pro-ducing a different kind of human being.

Second, *greater mobility*. The young man who so sincerely voiced himself as being so violently against violence flew across the continent to attend that meeting. In six hours he made a trip that would have taken the men who tried to analyze him four days in their youth. It would have taken their grandfathers four months. The impact of travel has always been life changing.

Third, *the loss of community*. Frequently we hear that change from the rural to the urban community is responsible for all our problems. It is not quite that simple. The real problem is the change from the unitary to the plural community, from the rela-tively simple community where the customs and ideals of the people were of all one kind to the complex community of com-munities with conflicting ideals and customs. In the simple com-munity adults and children tend to move toward each other and there is a kind of unstructured discipline administered by the community. In the complex overlapping communities adults and children tend to move away from each other and discipline is more the result of law than love.

The problem is not a simple one. The three underlying causes cited above only partly describe our dilemma. It is naive for one to fall into thinking that so complex a problem can be so simply described. For example, I know men who are broadly informed, widely traveled, and living in vast cities, who are about the sanest and most moral men I know; and I once lived in a com-munity isolated, ignorant, and intermarried that was just about the most violent community I ever knew. I would like, however, to propose that the right kind of communities are keys to a stabilized society, and that unless we find a way to reestablish community we will experience even more cultural shock.

This first came home to me when one of my sons and I were discussing some minor differences of opinion. He said in a moment of insight: "It bothers you that I don't think like you do, but why does that surprise you? I was always with other people more than with you, with my schoolmates, with my teachers, with my neighbor friends. After all you are but one of many influences in my life, and these other influences were often contrary to yours." I saw at once that values as I understood them were not being communicated to him as they had been to me. I had taken too much for granted. This set me to thinking about the nature of community and its bearing on our lives.

There are many communities to which each individual belongs. Take an average teen-age boy. First there is the community of his home to which he returns nightly. It may or may not be a community of love and learning. Too often it is little more than a place to sleep and eat and look at TV. Then there is the community of the schoolroom with a teacher and other youth, where learning is the stated purpose, and where the objectives may be quite different from those of the home. If the boy is an athlete, he belongs to still another community in which certain kinds of discipline are of highest importance. If he is a Boy Scout or motorcycle rider he belongs to still other communities of different standards and methods. If music is his thing, then he belongs to a "rock" or "country" community according to his tastes. If he is a church member, then he is part of the church community.

So much of the time these communities are hidden. They are not geographical, and they may not be identifiable. They often exist without formal structures and without recognized leaders. Tragically the parent is too often unaware of these communities and their influence on the child. Gradually the child begins to form a life style dominated by one of the hidden communities. The parent senses growing estrangement and begins to attack the child, not realizing the dominant influence of forces at work. Sometimes the parent does realize but too late to change the child. Values are learned very early in life or they are never learned at all, at least not without great trauma.

Sometimes parents are quite unaware of the effect of some of their own values which when carried to a logical end produce a certain level of character unanticipated. An American diplomat travels the world from one embassy to another priding himself on his world citizenship. His son caught his vision quite another way, and evaded his draft call by going to Sweden. He said: "I am a world citizen. The Vietnamese are my brothers. I will not fight them." His father's world views came home to him in quite a different way.

The conflicts of so many communities in the life of a child may create split personalities who belong to several and are at home in none. A Wall Street broker by day lives a conservative style of life, surrounded by others who appear just as conservative. With dark suit, white shirt, neatly cropped hair, he is in manner and word a most commendable businessman, but after office hours, he dons a wig and beads and takes his place as a member of the far-out. In both worlds he wears uniforms. In fact, the uniforms have a lot to do with making him what he is. Never really having found himself and having no true spiritual identity, he dons the uniforms and becomes an actor. His personal tragedy is the tragedy of so many people who have not been nurtured to maturity in a strong dominant community. They are divided and lost in worlds which offer them only surface identity. Deep down they do not belong anywhere and they have no name. The apostle Paul met a girl like this, a young woman whose life was a succession of images. So extreme and adept was she that evil men exploited her as a carnival freak. He saw her plight immediately. It does not take long for sensitive observers to discover the freakish nature of persons so divided and so immature that they cannot belong successfully to any community. In some ways all of us have divisions in our personalities, but the sick are those who have not found a dominating community that fosters healing and wholeness.

With the world in ferment and foment, one has to try very hard not to lose his own personal maturity and sense of relatedness. We feel much like a little four-year-old boy in the darkened Ford's Theater in Washington when the murder of Lincoln was being portrayed with sound and light. The cannons roared, men screamed, footsteps were heard walking toward the victim. Suddenly in the midst of the confusion the little boy cried: "Take me out of here." His world was black and he wanted out. Mr. Lincoln wanted out too. So did John Wilkes Booth. So do we. But the end of change is not escape or violence. Things never go back to the old way. The simple old communities are gone forever.

The answer is new kinds of communities in which responsibility for the race can be fully accepted. The call is for a renewal of the creative community of the church, for the church is the ultimate community to which a man must be related if there is to be total healing of the broken world.

Those of us who are Christians must take seriously the claim that Christ is the way, the truth, and the life for all men everywhere. We must make it clear that he has established a very special kind of community in which his love is nourished and communicated. This community, of course, is the church, sometimes called the body of Christ, and sometimes described as the people of God. For every Christian, the church is the dominant community, but never the exclusive community.

One reason some youth seem so little influenced by the churches in which they were reared is that they were never really committed to them. The ceremonies and rites were always conducted in such a way to isolate them from the congregation. Even the symbolism of their own baptism was made more a personal symbol than a symbol for their identity with the people of God. On the other hand, the reason these same young people identify with worldly communities offering false fellowship is that they make personal commitments to them, and through these commitments they become responsible for what happens to the groups. They become a member of the crowd. Because of very shallow concepts of Christian experience and Christian identification, our own youth too often live in our churches and in our homes without ever really being part of us. Nothing ever happens to give them any sense of responsibility to the community. Our hope as Christians is to return to an understanding of the church as community and to the realization that it can be creative community for all of its members.

The nature of true and false *koinonia* can be seen in the actions and attitudes of the sixteen-year-old girl who disappeared from her home and was finally found in a hippy community a thousand miles away where for weeks she had been living in a false aura of love and goodwill. Strangely her new found community accepted a reward of $1,000 to reveal her to her parents. The fellowship with which she was newly identified was false else there would not have been this betrayal. The fellowship in which she had been reared was genuine for she forgave her informants saying: "They needed the money." In the long run, we can hope and pray that the true fellowship to which she was never committed, though it did influence her, will win out over the false fellowship. This is always the hope of the creative Christian community.

The church is a creative community when it listens. Have you examined a red-lettered New Testament and seen how little talking Jesus did? There are some long passages, but much of the time he said only a few words and then listened. He listened to the sick and the blind, to sinners and publicans, to masters and servants, to children and adults, to rulers and the people. He was not a compulsive talker, one who had to say something to fill the silence or to speak to be heard. He could listen to words and he could listen to the absence of words, as when he knelt in the sand after he had said: "Let him that is without sin cast the first stone." Listening for him was a way of building confidence, of dispelling fear, and of validating himself. It was the dynamic half of communication. People came to him because he listened, as well as for what he said.

The church as community should have this same listening mind of Christ, both in a public formal way and in a private informal way. Its worship and learning services should be free and offer easy conversation and dialogue. Sensitivity to different insights and understandings should mark pastors as they listen to people and parents as they listen to children. Services should be structured to give people opportunity to share their problems and their concerns. None of this should take the place of preaching, for in the Christian service, preaching is preeminent, but even preaching should change to become more sensitive to the needs of the people and the whisperings of the Holy Spirit. It should be less polemical and more sensitive.

The creative church that listens will pay special attention to children and youth. It will remember their inability with words and feelings and that they can never truly say what they mean. It will recognize the symbolic nature of the things they say, and search beyond mere words for real feelings and convictions. The creative church will train its members to make friends with the dumb and to listen when no word is spoken. It will teach that every member has the responsibility for empathy with every other member, and for the whole world, and it will become known for the quality and depth of its empathy. The creative church will come alive in the lives of the people whom it hears, because as it listens in love and empathy it will be fulfilling the life and spirit of Jesus Christ. Listening, it will be the presence of Christ to the disturbed and the uncertain, the wicked and the wishful, and its listening will become the voice of God and sinners will hear and be healed.

The creative church is creative when it majors on spiritual values. A church has two ways to go, the way of things and the way of people. The further it departs from the New Testament, the more it will go the way of things. It will major on forms and ceremonies, and it will create symbols related to things. The ultimate surrender to things is seen in the pastor who said: "Our church is dead. The people are disinterested. We don't really need it, but we will build a building to revive them." This pastor had surrendered his ministry to a series of lifeless symbols of which the building was the most important one. I am not saying the building is unimportant, for as one who has worked with churches I surely know that buildings are extremely important. I am saying that it is possible to lose focus on the spiritual realities so that material things become all that one sees and understands.

We complain about the material symbols of the Roman Catholic Church, such as statues, candles, robes, chalices, vestments, and the like, all the paraphernalia that tends to mark that church more than its people. We assume our churches are free from similar symbols, yet I am not so certain.

For example, one pastor was frantic in trying to move the "Doxology" in the order of worship, and finally had to put it right at the middle. Many of the congregation could not worship if it were sung at the beginning. Almost none could worship when it was left out altogether; the "Doxology" had become a mighty symbol.

Another pastor believed he could communicate with people from a lower pulpit platform, especially on Wednesday nights, but when he tried to cut it down, the congregation was upset, for to them worship was not possible without a four-and-one-half-foot platform.

Another pastor resigned his church because his deacons would not recommend a divided chancel. He rigidly allowed his image of a divided chancel to become a symbol of church.

These are all minor symbols. Others include the way we conduct our meetings and when we have them. They include also such things as the church spires and Gothic windows, and perhaps colonial architecture. They include sizes of budgets, rates of increased enrolments, number of staff, ranks in the pipe organ, and many more things.

Again I am not saying that these are unimportant, only that they have tended to become the things people see when they think of us, like our thought of the Roman Catholics bring to mind all their paraphernalia. These visions tend to blur the church as community.

In the new times the creative church will shift its symbolism from the material to the spiritual, as it begins more seriously to identify with its own special mission. The light it sets on a hill will not be mere forms and ceremonies, but forgiveness and grace, humility and openness, understanding and empathy. The world will see its faith, hope, and love and be glad.

In Washington, D. C., the Windsor Hotel overlooks a little valley to the north of which is the great St. John's Cathedral. Early one morning I stood in a room high in the hotel looking at the darkened form of that cathedral in the shadows of early dawn. As I watched a transformation took place. The sky lightened and the side of the cathedral became a flaming golden fire, so bright I could scarcely see the building at all. It was as though it had suddenly started to burn. Then I realized what I saw was the reflection of the morning sun rising on distant rim of the valley against the great windows. Reflecting the sun the cathedral itself became alive and luminous. The glory of the church always becomes more glorious under the new light and new life of the rising Son of God. It is only as the community catches his light that it begins to live.

Churches sometimes try to find all their glory inside themselves by adding more paint and turning on more light bulbs. They must remember that their true glory comes as they reflect the light of Christ. Somehow they must return to his values and bear his spirit. The phrase "Living the Spirit of Christ" was never more important than now. The Master had a spirit different from all others, a healing spirit, a spirit of righteous indignation, a rugged yet kindly spirit, a demanding yet forgiving spirit, and a meek yet strong spirit. His spirit could drive out devils and quiet storms, attract little children and great lawyers, endure temptation and slander, and overcome suffering and death. The spirit of Christ was the spirit of profound love and loyalty, of enduring hope and faith and unswerving perseverance and victory. His spirit was the spirit of eternal life.

The creative church as a healing community will reflect this spirit, and suddenly will burn again and the world will see and sing anew its glories.

The creative church is creative when it is true to its mission. The true church is never wholly contained in an organization or a building. It is always more than a list of names meeting at a certain place. It is life going forth, it is ministry, it is leaven for the world. The church nevertheless is always gathering for worship where "festival and fantasy" are the mileu of its fellowship. This oscillation between involvement in life and separation for worship forms a dynamic community in which all who experience it are healed. The basic purpose is human redemption in keeping with God's plan of the ages that centered in Jesus Christ as the Savior of all men.

Some people hold that God keeps the universe moving through a process of explosion-implosion. Matter races toward matter until an incredible density is built up. The heat causes it to explode and stars and planets are born again. For endless milleniums it races outward until it spends itself and then it reverses once more to the center. A process of implosion-explosion takes place in the true church. The members come together where their fellowship with one another and with God gives them new impetus. They then explode into the world, each member following his own orbit and winning for Christ in whatever way he can. Spent, the members return again for the power they can gain from the heavenly community. Because their community is a community of Christ, their purpose always is to bring men unto that community, not merely by the formality of membership but by making them Christians.

The serious Christians of the world are beginning to realize again that the church has a unique mission to the world. I caught a glimpse of this new realization in a Sunday afternoon service in Westminster Cathedral in London. About a thousand worshipers sat in stiff high-backed benches and chairs where people have sat for about six hundred years. The clergy dressed in splendid robes of red and black and blue and gold came quietly down the aisle. The preacher, a professor of divinity from Oxford took his place and began to read his sermon. I was certain of a dull hour, but I was wrong. As he read, I felt a prophetic spirit: "The church," he said, "has done everything except what it was meant to do and what it alone can do. It has dabbled in political reform and been the handmaiden of kings. It has organized itself as a social enterprise, engaged in bazaars and raffles, fought wars and educated the general public. Sometimes it has done all this in the name of righteousness, and sometimes it has just done it. The time has come for the churches to see that they have one mission—making men Christians. It begins not with men, but with a man. It bears testimony of Christ to that man until he sees that his own responsibility to the world must start with himself as a Christian."

Always when I think about the church as Creative Christian community I come quickly to the concept of *koinonia,* the gathering, the fellowship, the family, the unique circle. The community must be both visible and invisible. It must move into the world of people to be diffused, but to become instantly alive and visible when one Christian meets another. The important thing is that this diffusion must always be related to what takes place when the church gathers.

One winter morning I stopped for worship at a small East Tennessee rural church. The pastor preached a very ordinary sermon and extended an invitation. After one or two stanzas of a hymn, he said something which I did not understand. At once people moved out of the pews to the front and stood around the pastor. Everyone in the room was in that circle except my wife and me and one other man. The singing stopped and he said: "Do you have anything you want to say to the church?" One man requested prayer for his wife, another told how the prayers of the church helped him find a job and a woman said: "I've had a problem which I could not discuss, but now I can thank God the patience and prayers of my friends in this church helped solve it." Another woman began weeping. She said: "I've done so wrong in my attitude toward some people in this church. I want their forgiveness and I want you all to help me have a right attitude." One rugged weather-stained farmwife said: "I am so happy I could shout"—and she did shout. Festival was present in that circle. Mystery was also present. It was a true communion of the saints. The thing that really interested me was the man who did not join that circle. He stood aloof and downcast. Two things were happening. The nature of the church as a separated community was being realized and a lost soul was struggling with the question as to whether or not he should take his place in that community. A few minutes later the benediction dismissed the community to the world. Wherever the members went, they carried the church. The *koinonia* was a living reality, the growing edge of the church, the presence of Christ in the world, the exploding community of creative righteousness.

CHAPTER 7

Creative Confidence

■ ■ ■

C. Oscar Johnson was a very famous preacher and pastor. His sermons were humorous, yet full of spiritual wisdom and power. His ministry so impressed a great city that his name was a symbol of leadership and honor. What is not always true was that C. Oscar Johnson was fully as great a Christian as he was preacher and pastor. He lived the spirit of Christ in relationship to all men. Once he was in an automobile wreck due to the carelessness of another driver. For weeks he lay flat on his back in a hospital bed. Some of his friends said he ought to sue the driver, but instead he called the young man to his bedside and witnessed to him. He refused to sue, deeming the soul of the man more important than any retribution. Oscar Johnson was no weak idealist, for he would have been the first to admit that there are times when men should be sued. His rule was always restraint in the name of Christ.

There are many modern men who live in the same spirit. One of them was sleeping in his camper when a car crashed into it and stopped six inches from his head. Most men would have been angry and immediately railed out at the driver. But not this man. He found him in a hospital and ministered to him. It turned out that the driver was despondent over losing his job and had been thinking about suicide. He was amazed at the camper whom he might have killed. "What kind of man are you? I nearly killed you, yet you talk to me about Christ."

There are people who would criticize these men as unrealistic. "They have no sense about the real world," they would say. "They are babes in the woods and don't know how to look after themselves." Admittedly, they do appear unworldly. Christian humility always looks like that, yet there was a time in America when most people were like them in mind and attitude. The spirit of Christ dominated most of the common people, even those who did not confess him or follow him. Men trusted one another because they believed in one another. They knew how to forgive and be forgiven. There was an enormous deposit of goodwill which provided a stabilizing influence. But today, much of the goodwill is gone, and we live in a nation dangerously near the brink. The symptoms of chaos and collapse are endless.

A young man living in a big city, must store his cameras and TV set with friends while he visits his parents, due to the high probability of theft. The area around the public library of another city is unsafe for women by day and for men by night. City after city reports graft in the police departments. Income tax evasion is at an all-time high. Big businessmen secretly defy the law to drive small businesses to the wall and increase their own profits. Drug addiction is increasing with the police apparently powerless in their efforts to dry up the sources.

Every conceivable kind of cure is being offered for these conditions: for burgulars, modern penal programs; for the dope addict, improved hospitals; for the policeman, higher salaries and better working conditions; for city crime, more housing and more jobs; and for the crime bill, better education and more recreation facilities. All of these are important, but the point of the New Testament is that as needful as these reforms are, something else is even more necessary.

The essential thing for all people everywhere and under all conditions is a right attitude toward other human beings. This does not derive from a plush bank account, a full stomach, a rich education, or a pure blood line. These may help, but the basic requirement is an inner poise and maturity. David recognized this long ago and prayed: "Create in me a clean heart, O God; and renew a right spirit within me." (Ps. 51:10). Jesus stressed the supreme value of this rightness with the words: "Blessed are the pure in heart: for they shall see God" (Matt. 5:8). Paul summed it up: "Now the end of the commandment is charity out of a pure heart, and of a good conscience, and of faith unfeigned" (1 Tim. 1:5).

The real peace of the land is not found in the number of policemen or the adequacy of the courts. Even if half our people were police officers and the other half judges, there would still be crime, perhaps, even rampant crime. The Old Testament clearly shows the inadequacy of law, and Jesus came not to supplant the law, but to show us a better way, the way of the clean heart and pure mind.

One of the basic scenes of the gospel took place in the night when one of the leading judges of the land came to Jesus to ask him some questions. Nicodemus said: "We know, Rabbi, that you are a teacher sent by God. No one could do the mighty works you are doing unless God were with him" (John 3:2, TEV). Jesus answered: "I tell you the truth: no one can see the kingdom of God unless he is born again" (3:3). Later he said to him: "Do not be surprised because I tell you, 'You must all be born again' " (John 3:7). In these words Jesus is speaking of the fundamental need of the human race, the need for interior cleansing.

There are three ways for man to live, inside the law, outside the law and above the law. Living narrowly inside the law can make men into feelingless robots. As a way of life it becomes a prison. In the end it deadens and destroys the soul of man. Living outside the law also destroys the soul of man. It is the way to chaos and destruction. Without law man soon is caught in the terrible lawlessness of the jungle. The end is total death.

Living above the law is the way of life. In this the law is not set aside. It is both our teacher and our judge, but by following the way of love and confidence the law becomes understandable, and in love and confidence man finds the power to do what many people wrongly think the law gives him power to do. The way of Christ enriches the law. It is founded on trust, and it guarantees what policemen and courts cannot guarantee, that all just laws will be obeyed and all unjust laws will be changed.

At the heart of everything Jesus said is trust. To be converted is to claim God's trust in oneself, and to establish one's trust in God. Involved in this transaction of trust between man and God is man's trust of other men. This is seen in the teaching of Jesus concerning gifts laid on the altar of God. "So if you are about to offer your gift to God at the altar and there you remember that your brother has something against you, leave your gift there in front of the altar and go at once to make peace with your brother; then come back and offer your gift to God" (Matt. 5:23–24, TEV).

Trust was basic in the attitude of C. Oscar Johnson toward the young man who caused him painful injury. The great Christian wanted to be at peace with all men. It was a requirement he felt necessary for acceptance before God. Trust was also basic with the camper. It was much more important to him that he have a good relationship with fellow human beings than it was to reap vengeance for the destruction of his trailer and the threat of his life.

Already I have said that to be converted is to claim God's trust in oneself and to establish one's trust in God. I want to show how this develops between God and man.

God says: "I believe in you." The plain truth of the matter is that from the foundation of the world God has gone to a lot of trouble to get man to see that he has confidence in him.

When God made Adam, he did four things to establish his confidence. First, he set him alone in the garden in the presence of the tree of evil, but he did not make him a puppet. There was no string tied to his hand to draw it back from the forbidden fruit. This was because God trusted him. Second, Adam had full responsibility for naming the animals. God drove them all by so he could see them, and whatever Adam named them was acceptable to the Lord. Third, when Adam finally ate the forbidden fruit and hid from God, the Lord found him, chastised him and set him outside the garden, but at the gate of the garden he placed the cherubim and the flaming sword "which turned every way, to keep the way of the tree of life" (Gen. 3:24). The cherubim and the sword formed a promise to Adam that someday he would reenter the garden. This was a promise of confidence, for despite Adam's wrongdoing, God still believed in man. Fourth, God told Adam to subdue all things, and to bring them under his feet. God still wanted Adam to see, that in spite of his wrong choices, he still trusted him with the world which he had made.

In all the years since God has dealt with man on the basis of trust. Take Moses, for example, an old man, eighty years old, a life failure, a common sheepherder, and living alone in the desert with his sheep. God confronted him with a command to go to Egypt and deliver the children of Israel from the bondage of Pharaoh. Moses viewed himself as a nothing and tried to evade God with four excuses. He said: "I have no authority, no stature, no talent, and others are better than I." But God would not listen to his excuses, and commanded him to go anyway. This was because God trusted him even when he didn't trust himself.

Elijah had a similar experience. He built a fire under the nose of Queen Jezebel. He did this to prove God's invincibility after the wicked queen had slain the prophets of the Lord. Enraged and defiant, Jezebel sent Elijah a message: "So let the gods do to me, and more also, if I make not thy life as the life of one of them by tomorrow about this time" (1 Kings 19:2). This frightened the mighty Elijah and he began running for his life. He ran for forty days and nights and finally fell exhausted in a cave. Like most other human beings, Elijah had come to the end of his rope. He imagined himself to be alone, deserted, and worthless. Yet the word of the Lord found him not in the wind, not in an earthquake, not in a fire, but in the hush of a still small voice. "Elijah, what are you doing here?" His reply was the reply of blindness and weakness. "Everything is lost, and only I am left." If Elijah could have his way, he would fade away into oblivion and we would never have seen him again. But God put steel into him. "Elijah, go back, go back to the wilderness of Damascus." When Elijah floundered around at the bottom of life, he found the Lord of life by his side, still believing in him and trusting him.

In the new Testament Simon Peter is also the object of confidence. Jesus found him in a boat by the seaside, failing as a fisherman, for he had fished all day and caught nothing. Jesus showed him that all he needed to do was to fish from the other side of the boat. A rough unlearned man with an explosive temperament and an impulsive spirit, Jesus saw in Peter something far greater than Peter saw in himself. Had it not been for the confidence Jesus had in him, he might have spent his life fishing from the wrong side of the boat. But the call, "Follow me, and I will make you a fisher of men," was the call of unreserved trust. Even though Simon Peter stumbled and fell many times, Jesus was always there to help him up. He knew Simon's weaknesses but he believed in him anyway. It was as though he said: "Simon, you are sand, but I am going to make of you a stone."

The greatest demonstration of God's hope for man is to be seen in Jesus Christ himself. If God had not believed in man and trusted man he would never have sent his only begotten Son to die for him. This supreme confidence is best seen in Paul's great summary of the gospel: "God commendeth his love toward us, in that, while we were yet sinners, Christ died for us" (Rom. 5:8). This was the greatest creative act of all time, and was the continuation of the initial act of creation. In a sense Jesus Christ is a second Adam. Through the first Adam, God gave mankind his image, through the second Adam, his Spirit. In the first Adam God deposited his hope for man, in the second the power to realize that hope. In the first Adam, God told physical man good-bye at the gate of the flaming sword. In the second Adam God told spiritual man good morning at the gate of the cross.

A young man without a television set determined to use his own mind to picture the things he would like to see. He formed a series of images that began with a man as totally physical, living by all things material, a grubby lowly being of earthy appetites, almost a completely nonspiritual being. Gradually his man changed from one image to another until he became a totally spiritual being, living outside his body and standing in the presence of God in the new garden of Eden and hearing God say: "Welcome home." This remarkable vision of a lonely young man without a TV set clearly pictures both the course of mankind through the ages, and the course of a single man who stands in Jesus Christ. This is probably what Paul meant when he said that in Christ we go from faith to faith and grace to grace. At the root of this progress are two things: One is that God created man to move from the lowest to the highest and the other is that because God believes that man is capable of this progress he makes it possible in Jesus Christ. Yet man always seems to hold back from the confidence of God. Like an automobile engine out of tune he is inclined to sputter along and finally die.

Man says: "I don't want you to believe in me." From the beginning man has resisted the trust God placed in him. Adam was the first. Even after God had put him in charge of all the animals and had given him the run of the garden, he rebelled by eating the forbidden fruit. He went further away from God by hiding in the woods and resisting the call of God. Cain also resisted God's confidence in him, first by refusing to believe that God would accept his gift and again by refusing to face up to his responsibility for his brother.

Moses is another good example of man's resistance to God's confidence. When the Lord spoke to him out of the burning bush and asked him to go back to Egypt and confront Pharaoh on behalf of the children of Israel, Moses began to try to evade the call. He offered four excuses. He said: "Who am I that I should go unto Pharaoh?" What he meant was: "I have no authority." God had to tell him that his presence with him was authority enough. Moses then said: "They will not believe me." In other words, "I am a little man, I have no stature." The Lord had to show him that the power of God was in his hand by turning of his staff into a serpent. Moses still resisted: "I am not eloquent." God had to remind him that after all he had made his mouth. Finally, Moses pleaded as so many other dodgers have pled: "Send, I pray thee, by the hand of him who thou will send." In other words, "Send someone else, send my brother Aaron." God's anger burned against Moses. He told him that he needed both of them and they would help each other.

God's anger always burns against evaders. He is never completely happy with any person who does not measure up to his fullest possibilities. When the Israelites complained in the desert, the anger of the Lord was kindled against them. (Num. 11:1). When Aaron permitted worship of the golden calf, God's anger burned, and Moses had to pray to save him (Deut. 9:19).

Once I saw in the face of an afflicted child all the emotions and self-righteousness of evasion. The child could hear and understand but could not talk. She had some affliction of the vocal cords. I was talking to her and her sister about Jesus. The sister left the room, and I was left face to face with this unfortunate girl. She was so skilful in her facial expressions and her body attitude that I could read her feelings. When I tried to tell her that God loved her and trusted her, she became proud, defiant, and finally walked from the room as a grand gesture of her independence from God. She never spoke one word, yet she resisted with all her might, the confidence of God.

Most of us can talk but we still do not put into words our evasions. We act in rebellion, boldly defying his love and his trust. Everything we do is an evasion, even our gestures. We evade God in so many different ways. For one thing, we refuse to see ourselves as we are. We invent fantasies about ourselves, living so to speak in a dream world, and viewing ourselves in a magic mirror that hides all the faults and blemishes. We do not repent, for we refuse to see anything wrong. We hide our true nature from ourselves, often without realizing that in hiding the bad, we hide also the good. The true self is never known, and therefore is not presented to God for cleansing. This is not merely an evasion of ourselves, but in reality, it is an evasion of God. We are afraid of ourselves and we are ashamed of ourselves. We realize that radical change must take place, but we are too proud and too vain to open the door to God's confidence. We evade him at the very seat of life, the place of the self.

We also evade God by being self-defensive. We try to justify all of our shortcomings and wrongdoings. From the inside we try to strengthen our lives by believing we are right in every decision. We cannot bring ourselves to admit any wrong.

Moreover, we evade God's confidence in us by rejecting his love. When Jesus asked us to go an extra mile with our brother, he was not asking us to do something that he would not do or that God had not already done. After all, God did commend his love to man by giving his Son to die for man. Jesus went the last mile to the cross without complaint or regret. His love is manifest everywhere in his life and in his word, yet we reject it by sometimes substituting things for it, but most of the time we reject it with a simple flat no. A young man I know, an adopted child, grew up doubting his parents loved him. He was twisted by polio and never being able to settle down in their love, he left home before he finished school. His life has been one lonely dreary failure for one reason: he could not accept the love of his foster parents.

Most of the personal tragedies of our times arise out of one thing—the loss of the sense of the love of God. To accept God as love is to accept the universe as friendly and to accept the end as triumphant. Evading that love is easy and many people do evade it, but they never know the transforming expectancy of great hope. If life gets rough—and for most people it does get rough—there is no victory and no triumph. The cost of evasion runs high.

God answers: "Nevertheless if you accept my confidence your life will be changed." It is a proven fact for most of us that when we begin accepting someone's confidence in us a transformation of life takes place. One man's childhood was attended by a series of personal failures. He entered a contest to win a *Book of Knowledge*. His essay was so bad the teacher would not send it in. He entered a poster contest and did not make even honorable mention. He tried for a life saving merit badge and failed. Later he tried for a prize awarded for the best declaration on "Why I Like My Hometown." It was dismal. His grades were poor and he was never appointed to any committees. The only elected office he held was vice-president of a Junior youth group. His last big effort was as debater in his senior year in high school. He debated five times and there were five decisions against his. The last debate was one he knew he would win. As he left home, his mother said: "You will win." At school Mr. Daniel Martin told him and his colleague "Have no fear, you will win." Mrs. George Lee, the coach, smilingly said: "Yes, you will win." But they lost without a single judge voting for them. His colleague faded into the night "to run his father's car into the flagpole." He hid behind the curtain and when everyone was gone crept out into the auditorium and into the front hall. Mr. Martin was still there: "Son, why are you here so late?" When he told him he said: "Never mind, young man, I have been watching you a long time and I believe in you." This was one of the the first times that anybody except his mother had ever said a personal word of confidence. At home, she repeated it. On Monday morning, Mrs. Lee repeated it again. Ever since he has been trying to win that debate. Years later Mr. Martin wrote him: "I believe in you just as I did the night you lost the debate." Mrs. Lee from an invalid's bed smiled and said: "I believe in you more than ever."

Somehow when strong people believed in me, I had to try to be what they thought I could be. The power of their confidence was greater than my failures. This, of course, is the meaning of the gospel. God says, "I believe in you," and begins to try to prove it to you, even to the extent of sending his Son to make the supreme sacrifice on the cross. He also says, "Accept my confidence and your life will be changed." If only every poor lost soul who flounders in self-pity and self-defeat behind his flimsy facades of pretended strength, but who underneath is afraid and incomplete could realize the meaning of God's simple message to him: "No matter how weak you are or how far astray you have gone, I still believe in you." Most people despise themselves because they have never realized that God has not rejected them. Parents may have rejected them, people may have rejected them, but not God. When they realize this, and respond to it, life immediately is better for them. Instead of moving from failure to failure they move from faith to faith.

This is what salvation is—God and man moving into mutual confidence in each other. First God moves toward man. He does this in many different ways, but mostly through the coming of Christ to the world and his participation in its tragedies and its death. Through his Spirit, he issues an invitation to man. God's confidence has been fully proved. It is now up to man to establish his confidence in God. He must move in simple trust toward God. His movement is in two simple steps. In one he turns his back on wrong and in the other he puts his faith in Christ. The transaction is complete the moment he begins to live as though the confidence and love of God are truly meant for him.

One of the mysteries of the gospel is that God cannot give the individual the power for change without that individual's personal response. Another mystery is that the individual cannot move toward God until he realizes that God truly believes in him. The meeting of the two confidences in surrender to each other is the salvation experience. When this happens one is born again. He moves into a new dimension of life—the spiritual dimension where purity of heart and mind become the controlling factor in his relationships to all people. His values change and he begins to see that life on this planet is not possible without trust of man in God and of men in other men. He moves clumsily into his new life, making many mistakes, and frequently stumbling. Yet he somehow emerges from his fallings a little more trusting and a little more trustworthy. Finally he finds his completeness in Christ.

I started this chapter by describing the attitudes and actions of two men who out of pure hearts dealt with people who had wronged them. They were acting as men of trust, and having caught the spirit of Christ, they imparted something of that spirit in their dealings with fellowmen. They became true ministers of Christ to their enemies. Both sacrificed something in order to keep the Christian hope alive. They became true peacemakers, considering themselves expendable when a gap stood between themselves and other men.

A Christian stands in a gap between all the warring elements of this world to keep them from burning each other up and to secure union between them. He does this by accepting God's trust in him and by trusting other people. This, of course, is creative confidence.

CHAPTER 8

Expectant Faith

■ ■ ■

Have you ever made an inventory of your life's fears? Have you dared to set down on paper all the things you've been afraid of, from your earliest memory until now? Try it sometime. You will be surprised both as to its length, and at the emotions that memory stirs up within you.

Consider one man's fears. His first remembered fear was of dogs. Later came a fear of bridges and of deep water. Very early in life he developed a fear of people, especially of strange women. Almost as deep was a fear of the end of the world. Once when an oil tank burned beyond a distant hill, he was frantic until he learned that the world was not burning. Then came fear of surgical operations, especially appendectomies. Hospitals were always frightening to him, and many a time he walked on the opposite side of the street to avoid them. If the surgery windows were lighted, he would run until out of sight. School examinations were terrifying, and he came to the end of every school year awfully afraid that he would fail. He would put off going for his report card to the last possible minute fearful that he had not been promoted.

In his teen years his fears multiplied. He developed deep fears of war and unemployment. A nagging fear of heart trouble became an obsession which followed him most of his life. It started when his parents made him wear the corduroy trousers and brown sharp-toed shoes of his cousin who had died of congenital heart disease. His deepest fear was that his father would die.

In these sensitive years he was afraid that he might not be saved, and afraid he would miss the will of God. In depression and poverty he was afraid he might not get an education. He was also afraid he might marry the wrong girl.

Gradually a transformation took place in his fears. His earliest fears were of what might happen to him, but his later fears were of what might happen to others and to the cause to which he had given his life, fears for his wife and children, fears for the people he served and the work he did, fears for the community and the nation, fears that somehow the world might miss the way and end in terror.

This long list of fears might lead you to think that this man lived out his years in morbid pessimism. Not at all, for there were a great many things of which he was not afraid; and even the things he feared became a challenge to him. They inspired in him a special kind of power with which to deal with them. He learned very early in life that it never helps for one to run from the things he fears. He faced his fears and conquered most of them. He found that proper confession of fears can be cleansing, and that it is a prerequisite for strength.

Fear is a big part of the reality of life. It is present in almost every human situation. The person who says, "I have never been afraid," is either completely blind to his own nature or he is not telling the truth. Fear lies at the heart of almost every human activity. It is especially present in our excesses. The man who works too hard may be motivated by a deep fear of failure. The person who tries to excel his brothers in piety or virtue is often pushed along by a fear of temptation or a fear of some secret inner weakness. The young person who fights for his hippy hair, frayed jeans, and bare feet is frightfully afraid he will not be accepted by his chosen peer group. His parents who object to these things may be afraid of the criticism of their peer groups.

It is hard for man to escape his fear, for the truth is, he does not have fear, but fear has him. Fear swallows him, and the noise of fear drowns out his ears until he is reduced to almost a nothing. His fear makes him seem smaller and smaller even to himself. He runs, but fear follows him. He denies fear but it reappears to accuse him. He kicks it in the teeth, only to have it kick back and cut him in two, and he becomes more than one person, a divided personality. His fear is as big as his sin, perhaps bigger than his sin, perhaps even it is his sin.

Men are afraid for many reasons. One, they are afraid because of ignorance. The teen-ager was afraid of heart trouble, and it was not until he learned all about the heart and its strengths and weaknesses that he ceased to be afraid. The child was afraid the world was burning up until his father showed him that it was an oil tank afire. The child was also afraid of bridges until he began to study how bridges were made and what held them together. Most fears are dispelled when the facts are known. However, men sometimes are afraid because they do know the facts. A merchant knows the raw facts of his depleted inventory, his cost of sales, his declining profits, his lack of customers and he is afraid. But even here it is better to face the facts than to ignore them, for knowing them one can discover how to deal with them.

Again, men are afraid because of sin in their lives. Sin and fear are frequently the opposite sides of the same piece of cloth. Wherever one appears, the dye from the other side soon eats through. Peter denied Jesus Christ, his Lord, and was afraid. Adam ate the forbidden fruit and was afraid. Cain killed Abel and was afraid. Of course, some men sin, and pretend not to be afraid, but it is only a pretense. They may not know of their fear, but deep inside holiness is destroyed, and where there is no holiness there is no wholeness. Without wholeness life can be only partially lived, fear is inevitable. Yet if one will confess his sin, his fear may disappear.

Also, men are afraid because they have not found their own special truth. They are attempting to live the truth of other people, or they are living by outright lies. They are many people, not just one person. There is no internal spiritual stability, no psychological maturity. They are governed by their prejudices, not by their principles. So many of the youth of today live on philosophical crumbs borrowed from one another, a half-truth here, a snatch of truth there, a lie here, a whim there, and so on until as one of them said they are just a collection of hollow mirrors. Discovery of my own special truth is one of the most creative things that can happen to me, for there suddenly where I find my truth I find God's will for my life, and fear is driven away. There is no truth without God at the other end of it.

Finally, men are afraid because of their lack of faith. The tragedy of fear is that it tends to build up what it is afraid of. My experience in public speaking has proved this to me again and again. For many years I have had to address a great many audiences of different sizes and moods. As a successful public speaker my "batting average" is less than 500 percent, which in the baseball world would be a good score, but in public speaking, it is not so good. I've noticed that when I fear an audience, I freeze and fail. The more afraid I am, the higher the probability of failure. I am like the high hurdle runner who keeps looking back because he is afraid of the next runner or the tightrope walker who forgets the rope and looks at the ground. There is a dilemma here, for in spite of himself, even the most successful speaker will be afraid of his audience and the most successful runner will be afraid of losing the race. The opposite of fear is not courage. Indeed it is possible to have both fear and courage at the same time. The true opposite of fear is faith. Courage without faith is both meaningless and impossible. Men without faith are doomed to finally fall victim to their fears, no matter how much personal courage they have.

People handle different fears in different ways. Some give up to fear. They are overwhelmed and destroyed by the things of which they are afraid. A woman has a domineering inconsiderate husband. He is mean and selfish, and at times violent. She retreats into her innermost self, cringing, apologetic and spiritless. Her personality degenerates until she is only a shadow of her true self. Other people try to repress their fear, and begin to live superficial and artificial lives. They become detached from reality, assuming a poise or an attitude which cannot be defended, yet they defend it with all their might. Still others meet fear with faith. They face their fears honestly, turning them around and around before their eyes, carefully analyzing them and understanding them, all the while keeping optimistic and hopeful. Instead of looking for the worst, they look for the best. Instead of cringing in the shadow of fears, they climb on top of them.

Expectant faith reaches for reality it cannot see. I once owned a little dog that seemed afraid of everything. The slightest voice in the yard would send him into loud barking. A stranger would cause him to tremble and whine. A move of the hand as though to strike him would make him bristle and bark. As this dog grew older his fear turned to aggression. He would snap or bite at any stranger and even at those who tried to help him. Finally we had to put the dog in a pet shelter. His fears had made him completely unsuitable for living in a normal home situation.

The trouble was that the dog had somehow missed reality. Nobody wanted to hurt him. He had never been threatened with a stick or a stone, yet he could not sense that he was among friends who did not want to harm him. I don't know what made that dog blind to the reality of his friendly world. In the case of human beings, I think that refusal to face reality is the lack of simple basic faith. Dogs live by fear; humans ought to live by faith.

Some young people in high school and college are frightfully afraid of examinations. They put them off as long as they can rather than run the risk of failing. Others ridicule psychological tests, calling them silly and superficial, not because they can prove these charges, for they cannot. Their real problem is that they are afraid of seeing the reality of their own psychological profile. People without faith, don't know that it is better to fail an examination than run away from it and better to live by truth than by error. Facing and failing the test of reality is faith, and as paradoxical as it sounds, it is also victory. Running from reality is doubt, and means final defeat.

Faith in God as a God of love is affirmation that one believes all existence to be a friendly existence. He admits that in his personal existence pilgrimage there are ups and downs and all kinds of deterrents, but at the end there is the crown of life. He believes that under God all the ups and downs work together for good. For the true believer there is hope in the darkest night. If he lives by faith, he finds the momentum of life's adventure strong and sustaining, but if he lives by fear momentum is lost and life becomes deadly boredom. By faith he rises to excellence, by fear he lapses to mediocrity.

Many Christians have not learned what it means to live without fear. They have forgotten that the Bible is a book of courage and faith, and that from beginning to end it offers victory to people who face reality. The promises of God leap at us. "Fear thou not; for I am with thee: be not dismayed; for I am thy God: I will strengthen thee; yea, I will help thee; yea, I will uphold thee with the right hand of my righteousness" (Isa. 41:10). The confessions of faith that rise above fear are most inspiring. "God is our refuge and strength, a very present help in trouble. Therefore will not we fear, though the earth be removed, and though the mountains be carried into the midst of the sea" (Ps. 46:1–2). "The Lord is my light and my salvation; whom shall I fear? The Lord is the strength of my life; of whom shall I be afraid?" (Ps. 27:1).

Jesus himself enforces again and again the need for faith to overcome fear. "Fear not, little flock; for it is your Father's good pleasure to give you the kingdom" (Luke 12:32). "Let not your hearts be troubled: ye believe in God, believe also in me" (John 14:1). "Let not your heart be troubled, neither let it be afraid" (John 14:27).

John the apostle on Patmos saw a vision of Christ standing in the midst of lampstands, eyes like fire, voice like the sound of many waters, and his face shining like the sun. John fell down as though dead. Then John said, "But he laid his right hand upon me, saying, 'Fear not, I am the first and the last, and the living one; I died, and behold I am alive forevermore, and I have the keys of Death and Hades' " (Rev. 1:17–18, RSV).

All these passages have several things in common. They suggest that faith helps man find the truth in the harshest realities of life, and they reassert God as friendly to man; they offer God as both the object and means of faith, and they offer faith as an alternative to fear.

Some people live with their backs to life; they just cannot face things as they are. They are perfect examples of the truth of the old saying: "Nothing ventured, nothing gained." They forget that they are men and women of the world, called upon to venture forth into the world. It would be far better for them to be Don Quixote fighting windmills and dreaming impossible dreams than to live with their backs to windmills and dreams. The glory of Don Quixote was that in his dying moments what had seemed to be a dream turned out to be not a dream at all, but reality. That is our glory too, if we dare to believe and try. Enoch believed and tried and was caught up to heaven. Noah believed and tried and became a doer of righteousness. The writer of the Hebrews said: "These all died in faith, not having received what was promised, but having seen it and greeted it from afar, and having acknowledged that they were strangers and exiles on the earth. For people who speak thus make it clear that they are seeking a homeland. If they had been thinking of that land from which they had gone out, they would have had opportunity to return. But as it is, they desire a better country, that is, a heavenly one. Therefore God is not ashamed to be called their God, for he has prepared for them a city" (Heb. 11:13–16, RSV). People who look back in fear will die in fear. People who look forward in faith will triumph in faith.

I have said that we ought to believe and try. To some this may not be theologically correct, for work ought not to be any part of faith. Certainly faith to be pure must stand alone, but faith without works alongside is dead. Belief without effort is also dead. The dreams of so many of us perish because we are not as willing as Noah and Abraham to look ahead and act decisively on the assurance of faith that beyond our vision God stands, ultimate truth and reality.

Some would condemn the working out of dreams as worldly and unchristian. It may be worldly in a sense, but not unchristian. We may have failed to see that we must live our Christian lives in the world. We are to subdue the earth, to find its truth and reality, not as people belonging to the world but as to God. Paul Tournier speaks to us in wisdom:

> "Faith, far from turning us away from the world brings us back to it . . . awakens in us a new interest in the world, in the concrete reality of every day, hard, laborious, difficult, often painful to us, but wonderful nevertheless. The joy of living, of making an effort, of having a goal to aim at: the joy of moving a finger, of smelling a perfume, of looking at something, of hearing a voice, of learning something and loving someone. The pleasure of research, of success, of study; the pleasure of discovery, of the excitement with a difficult problem, the pleasure of understanding something one did not understand before, of knowing what one did not know, the pleasure of the puzzle of its solution. . . . The joy of feeling that what I do at each moment is absolutely unique that no one else will ever be me, that every moment in my life will be the same as this one. The joy of each experience, of each act, of each success, as soon as we realize that this is what is meant by being in God's image, that he allows us to cooperate in his work, that he is with us in everything we undertake. It is from him that we draw our courage to live." [1]

Expectant faith helps us discover unexpected sources of strength. This long passage by Paul Tournier from his book *The Adventure of Living* means one thing: God is our helper. This also is the message of the New Testament. God is always in the shadows of life to help those of us who need him, yet he does not enter our lives against our wills. He moves providentially in the lives of all people, but consciously only to those who accept him. The experience of God as helper comes only to men and women of faith. There is a sense in which faith can be defined as the personal recognition of the action of God in our lives.

Jesus makes very clear the place of faith in the life of the Christian. He asked his disciples who were afraid of the storm: "Why are ye so fearful? O ye of little faith" (Matt. 8:26). He told blind Bartimaeus that his faith had brought him a personal victory. "Go thy way; thy faith hath made thee whole" (Mark 10:52). He tried to show the disciples the power of faith. "If ye had faith as a grain of mustard seed, ye might say unto this sycamine tree, Be thou plucked up by the root, and be thou planted in the sea; and it should obey you" (Luke 17:6). Receiving is contingent on asking: "Ask, and it shall be given you; seek, and ye shall find; knock, and it shall be opened unto you" (Matt. 7:7).

Paul calls faith one of the three great spiritual gifts, the other two being hope and love. He said: "I can do all things through Christ which strengtheneth me" (Phil. 4:13) and "But my God shall supply all your need according to his riches in glory by Christ Jesus" (Phil. 4:19). He said that the worthy Christian is one who is "strengthened with all might, according to his glorious power" (Col. 1:11). These few passages which could be multiplied many times show the place of faith in bringing God's power into our lives.

The mystery of faith is that it means unlimited life all at once. Through faith we are suddenly in touch with the eternal; it is to live an eternity now. Faith is not merely the way we come to eternal life, it is eternal life.

Yes, faith brings power into our lives, not because it possesses some special magic of its own, but because the other end of it is always fixed upon God. Most of us sooner or later are broken in one way or another. When we are broken, one of two things happens: Either the break does not heal and we are defeated in spirit, or the break heals and we are stronger than ever in the broken part. The difference is in the presence of faith. The weakling will never stand again on his broken heart for fear it will break again. The man of faith takes his place in eternity, a place promised only to the faithful, and stands not on the weakness of his broken heart, but on the strength of God's response to his faith.

Expectant faith releases life to rise above limitations. There is no such thing as the perfectly endowed or totally adequate person. List ten people, and you will have written down ten differents sets of curious combinations of abilities and shortcomings. List a hundred people and you will have a hundred sets. A few of the hundred may see themselves as complete personalities. These are the unfortunate ones. Being too sure of themselves they are destined for mediocrity. People who have no uneasiness about themselves cannot possibly judge themselves in relation to reality. They are bound to fail.

I have taken all these words to say that nearly everyone has an inferior complex, and that they are better off for it. This is surely true provided they get it under control and do not go to the extreme of constant self-depreciation. This too spells defeat and is fully as bad as the extreme of too much confidence. Between these two extremes of excessive self-confidence and self-condemnation the battles of life take place and most people finally win lasting victories.

People with inferior complexes—and this includes most of us—secretly imagine they bear blemishes and scars deeper than those of other people. They sometimes brood over these shortcomings until they see nothing else. The richest ones of them may be richly endowed, with plenty of capabilities on which life can be built, but they are fascinated with capabilities they don't have, and they spend a great deal of time trying to be something they can't be.

People who have best won the battle of the inferiority complex have discovered their strength comes from God. The best thing to say to a person of no self-confidence is what he cares the least about hearing and is most apt to ignore. It is, "Put your faith in God." Faith is the weapon one must ultimately use against his self-doubt and self-destruction.

Take the alcoholic as an example. Basically his problem is failure. He is sick with self-disgust. The history of alcoholism shows that it is practically impossible for the person to cure himself through willpower. Within himself there is utterly no strength. Alcoholics Anonymous has shown that strength comes when the alcoholic begins to live outside himself to find strength in his friends and in his God. The healing comes through faith. It is strange that the world does not understand or hear this, but then it has often ignored Jesus who said, "Thy faith hath made thee whole." People whose lives are made whole by faith are consistently victorious even when they lose.

A man I know had two little boys who had diabetes. Both cases were extremely irregular and severe. They did not respond consistently to insulin, and in those days diabetic diets were very hard to control in children. The parents were frantic in search of a miracle. I remember driving with this father from Texas to West Virginia in search of a doctor who was said to have found an herb that would cure the disease.

The youngest child lived until he was a senior in high school and died one day after having been struck suddenly blind. The other boy lived until he was married and had a child of his own. What made it doubly hard was that the parents knew that most diabetics live long normal lives, yet every day the symptoms for their sons seemed to point in the other direction.

In the midst of all his suffering I went to talk with this father about a personal problem of mine that for me seemed very serious. He listened with deep sincere interest and then he said: "My friend, you must work at your problem. You must try every door and think deeply to find a solution—but if you don't find it, you must be quiet in your faith in God. You must go to your knees and deliver everything into his hands. He can give you peace and victory even though you lose everything."

This man has consistently been one of the really radiant Christian lights of my experience. He has been tremendously effective in the pulpit. His crowning work was the college classroom where he taught the Bible to hundreds of young men and women. They remember him for the overflowing fulness of his faith. He is not what you would call a man of great piety yet he breathes the spirit of prayer and faith into everything he touches.

In his retirement this man has continued his testimony of the faithful life, helping churches and ministers wherever he can. He has a hobby that takes him into the western hills in search of gem stones. With these little treasures of God's great storehouse he makes beautiful jewelry for his family and his friends. Many a time I have followed this man in my imagination through the hills, digging, scooping, and hammering; and later at home with his saw and polisher, his forceps and his torch. This friend is a man of contentment because he is a man of faith.

NOTES

1. Paul Tournier, *The Adventure of Living* (New York: Harper, 1965), p. 237.

CHAPTER 9

Expectant Hope

■ ■ ■

In western Tennessee and Kentucky two great rivers flow side by side for almost fifty miles. They are from five to fifteen miles apart, and between them are thousands of acres of gentle sloping hills covered with wide meadows and beautiful woods. For more than 150 years hardy farmers tilled these lands and built on them their houses and villages. Fences were straight and strong, houses and barns in good repair and well painted and schools and churches well kept and attractive. One day there came the news that a government agency was buying up the land to build a park. At first people refused to believe it and went about their tasks as usual. But as farm after farm was sold, and the tide ran against all efforts to keep the old communities intact, despair took hold of the hearts of the people. Gates sagged, fences fell down, planks fell off barns, houses were left unpainted and cemeteries overgrew with weeds and honeysuckle. People looked around them and said: "It's no use."

A traveler stopped for gasoline at one of the last filling stations to remain open. Only one pump was working and the attendant was moody and disinterested. "What's wrong?" the traveler asked. He waited a long time to answer. A piece of loose tin on the roof banged in the wind. Finally the man said: "Mister, there is no hope, and when hope dies, a body loses his power to do."

This, of course, is the story of a great many people in the

world, hope has died and they have lost their power to do. Without expectant hope there can be no lasting personal victory of any kind. Long ago Samuel Johnson said: "Where there is no hope, there can be no endeavor."

Hope is hard to define. It perhaps can better be described. One man called it a waking dream and another, the parent of faith. Others have said hope was the only cheap and universal cure, a patent medicine for disease, disaster, and sin. Emily Dickinson said: "Hope is the thing with feathers—that perches in the soul." George Herbert called it "the poor man's bread." One of the best descriptions is also from Samuel Johnson: "Hope is itself a species of happiness, and perhaps the chief happiness which this world affords."

The most miserable people on earth are those who can see nothing ahead. Men who live without hope are the true poor people of the world. They are the hollow people whose days are like empty boxes laid end to end, and the older they get the more those boxes look like caskets, until one day one of them is a casket. If hope is the promise of a glorious sunrise that is to come, then the absence of hope is the experience of a bitter night already taking place.

Men can despair over many things, themselves, the people about them, the conditions of the world and finally what to them is the meaninglessness of life. Perhaps the bitterest despair of all is the despair of being themselves. Soren Kirkegaard called this kind of despair the sickness unto death. Men look at themselves and what they see they don't like. The harder they try the more hopeless they feel. They "cop out" on life. Some commit suicide, others become social vegetables, functioning in the world but never being true to themselves. Still others become tramps and vagabonds, now known as hippies. Most keep on living in this narrow little world, trees without roots, clouds without rain, wells without water, "having no hope, and without God in the world" (Eph. 2:12).

One does not need to be a hippy to cop out on life. But

whether one is hippy or not, the causes are the same, sickness unto death, the despair of self, the unwillingness to be the soul God made. The cry for attention so many of these people make is an empty carnival cry, the wail of a show barker who calls the people to come and see the tatooed lady. When we look, we see an unfortunate woman who to find herself hid herself with ugly lines and drawings. The people who so desperately adorn themselves with all kinds of bizarre decorations are trying to hide the self God gave them and meant for them to live with.

Why do they do this? Why are they not willing to accept themselves for the person God made them and seek his glory for their lives? For one thing, they make a personal idol of their idealized selves. They see themselves as being wiser, braver, prettier than they are, and the more they try to live by their perfections the greater their sense of imperfection. Also, they are never able to get the internal and external forces of their lives working together. Most of them live with their personal center of gravity totally outside themselves. The youth mad about race cars and the man mad about walking horses are examples. They have not seen that God comes to man as a still small voice within, and that what is on the inside must find harmony with the outside. The longer we put off reconciliation, the deeper we move into despair. Furthermore, man wishes always to evade responsibility. He does not want to get caught in the "nine to five rat race" or any other kind of trap. He despairs because he will not face responsibility, claiming that responsibility interferes with his freedom. What he does not see is that true freedom is freedom *in* responsibility, not freedom *from* responsibility. Finally, man stubbornly holds out against God, ignoring him or cursing him or dismissing him as dead. He does not believe because he dares not believe, and he dares not believe because he has no hope. For modern man it is not God who is dead, but hope. The coils of nihilism tighten around his soul, for without hope he cannot believe God and without God he cannot have hope.

Man sometimes despairs over people and the condition they create in the world. This can range from the hopelessness a mother feels whose sons all go to jail or whose daughters all take up dope, to the helpless frustration a father feels when a raging social revolution turns his world upside down. Mothers like this have been known to lose their sanity and fathers to commit suicide.

We despair over people who choose the things that will destroy them or who live by values different from ours. We despair over conditions that threaten our security and which disturb the world. The bitterest despair comes when we fail in our assumed role of playing God to people and events. We try to control them and cannot. Being human our disappointment is about as much with ourselves in our lack of omnipotence as it is in the persons and conditions we try to control. Hope fails because it is grounded in self.

Some people despair over what to them is the meaninglessness of life. Either they look forward to life and conclude it useless, or they look back at life and conclude it empty. Not all people go this far—some of them because they find faith that gives life meaning, some because they don't think deeply about life, and others because they reach despair long before they ever consider the question of life's meaning. A man worried about where his next meal is coming from may not have time to think about why he lives and what is the end of it all. But the people who do despair over the meaning of life know an emptiness and a frustration not understandable to the rest of us. Their despair is the other side of faith, a black desperate doubt that destroys their ability to function as normal persons.

This then is our task, the universal restoration of expectant Christian hope. Erich Fromm has said: "To hope means to be ready at every moment for that which is not yet born, and yet not become desperate if there is no birth in our lifetime." [1] Now, while I would not agree with all the conclusions of this writer, I find nothing wrong in these words. He also said: "Hope is the mood that accompanies faith. Faith could not be sustained without the mood of hope. Hope can have no base except faith." [2]

The hope I am writing about is not the mood of optimism, the effervescent expectancy that somehow things are going to get better and better. Part of what is wrong with so many religious experiences is a surrender to a heedless hope which can be compared to an electric blanket that warms as long as the switch is on and the current is running. Nor is the hope I am writing about a general mood of goodwill that prevails among all human beings, a kind of humanistic certainty.

Expectant Christian hope lies much deeper. It grounds in God as the friendly God of love, the Father of us all, the searching Shepherd, who works ceaselessly to close the gap between himself and man. The Scriptures make the place and ground of his hope clear. The preacher promised us: "For to him that is joined to all the living there is hope" (Eccl. 9:4). The psalmist cried: "Why art thou cast down, O my soul? and why art thou disquieted in me? hope thou in God" (Ps. 42:5). In the New Testament the emphasis on hope is ever plainer. "Blessed be the God and Father of our Lord Jesus Christ [who] . . . begotten us again unto a lively hope by the resurrection of Jesus Christ" (1 Pet. 1:3). As Christians, "Ye sorrow not, even as others which have no hope" (1 Thess. 4:13). The Scriptures were "written for our learning . . . that we through . . . the scriptures might have hope" (Rom. 15:4). J. Wallace Hamilton puts it: "The gospel of Christ came as the good news of hope. It had a hopeful view of God, a hopeful view of man and a hopeful view of history. History is not just going around and around. It is moving toward a goal. The goal is the kingdom of our God and his Christ." [3] The Christian who lives by expectant hope keeps an open door to miracles, an open heart to victory, and an open hand to action.

Expectant faith keeps an open door to miracles. Our age is one in which most people both strongly accept and reject the possibility of miracles. They find it easy to believe that man will someday move from planet to planet as he now moves from country to country and to believe that cures will be found for such diseases as cancer and heart trouble.

Man's belief in his miracles is based on his confidence in his own powers. In a sense he has made a god of himself, a miracle-performing god who always is doing the impossible. His special omnipotence is science, and with science he believes anything can be thought, any problem solved, any secret discovered. In short, he believes that anything that needs to be done can be done. He believes this because he has developed a kind of religious feeling about science, an unashamed confidence in its invincibility. Even school boys and novices who do not understand the scientific processes talk glibly of the day when they will travel to the stars. They are caught up in a great compulsion to take by faith and hope what they do not understand. They have simply transferred their religious faith from the spiritual world to the material world.

These same people vehemently reject spiritual miracles. It is incredible to them that there is a form of spiritual reality transcendental to material reality. They denounce miracles of love and faith as superstition, not realizing what the true believer knows, that beyond and above the material realm is a spiritual realm vaster than all the stars and as deep as the human heart itself. The kind of miracles one should expectantly look for are as numerous as people, so I will point out only three basic ones.

First, there is the miracle of God himself. Most people who escape God think of him as power or principle or law, even as routine force that does not matter because it changes not. They fail to see him as a loving, living, creating Father whose mind thinks and whose heart feels and whose will acts. They fail to see him as closer to themselves than their shadows, and as always lifting them out of trouble and shielding them from ruin.

The God of the Scriptures is the God whom imagination cannot improve or our thinking conceive or touch. Without him there would be no human existence, human knowledge or human goodness. Contrasted with all the evil and uncertainty of the world, our God is a miracle God. As John Baille put it, "God is He with whom we have ultimately to do, the final reality to which we have to face up, and with whom we have in the last resort to reckon."

That God lives where we cannot see him, that he spans all time and all space, and that he has our interest at heart, all this is a miracle. The destructive despair of our day arises out of hearts who have missed God. To them he is incredible. Their deliverance is to hope for the miracle of his existence. The alternative is total and absolute destruction and what is worse the complete failure of self-realization, for without God the plant does not bloom and personality does not find its completion. Without God all things dry up and blow away.

Second, there is the miracle of God in your life. It is one thing to see the rainbow, but it is quite another different thing to have a rainbow in your heart. It is the same with God. Seeing him at a distance is a great experience; knowing that he has come to live with you is incomparably greater. This, of course, is what Christianity is all about. After all the name of our Savior is Emmanuel or "God with us." Jesus Christ put the idea into a few short wonderful words. In his great prayer he said: "The glory which thou gavest me I have given them. . . . I in them, and thou in me" (John 17:22,23). The miracle is God with us in Jesus Christ. Most people cannot accept the miracle of God in their lives because they are caught up too much in the world, even to the point of seeing God and the world as against each other. They cannot accept one without letting the other go. There is a sense in which this is true for no man can serve God and mammon. Yet Jesus said in that same prayer: "As thou hast sent me into the world, even so I also sent them into the world" (John 17:18). He made the world and all things in it, and from the beginning it has been God's will for men to subdue the world. The miracle then is the fusing of the world and God in my experience of Jesus Christ.

Third, the miracle of the forgiveness of your sins. When a prominent American author died at seventy-three, they found her on the floor of her disordered room amidst empty liquor bottles and dog litter. Whiskey, drugs, and profligacy had at last destroyed her sensuous body and brilliant mind. Talented in the use of words and at writing and owning a unique beauty she threw it all away in exchange for a few brief thrills until at last she was a demented dirty old woman, rejected and forgotten. One wonders about her real sin. Was it pride? Was it egotism? Was it godlessness? Was it the disposition to play god to people and events around her? Or was it that she was like so many others, a child of the world around her?

Whatever it was, you can be sure that she waited all of her life for a miracle that never came, the miracle of the forgiveness of sin. Her unforgiven sin was the heaviest load she had to bear and she apparently never got rid of it.

Most people are destroyed by their unforgiven sin. Some are crushed, others are twisted and deformed and others slowly die without knowing the sin they die of. Sin marks them with a deep hunger for its cure; yet not knowing how they can escape, they dare not hope. They may not die in a room of whiskey bottles and dog litter, but the effect is the same, for the debris of their sin is in their own souls. They die, tormented on the inside, having never experienced forgiveness of their sin. They need to see that "now, in Christ Jesus, ye who sometimes were far off are made nigh by the blood of Christ" (Eph. 2:13). They need to know the great assurance of the forgiveness of their sins.

Expectant hope keeps an open hand for action. One of the saddest pictures in the world is to see a man who hopes but does not reach out to make his hopes come true. When James said: "Faith without works is dead," he surely meant that any kind of a spiritual attitude that is not matched with some kind of human effort is meaningless. Hope that does not try is not hope at all, but abject surrender to whatever happens. A father hopes his child does not die of diphtheria, but refuses to take it to a physician; a mother hopes her daughter will marry well, but never tries to teach her proper values and good attitudes. A student hopes he passes the test, but refuses to study. A man hopes he gains eternal life, but refuses to enter into conversation with God. Passive hope is not Christian hope.

Do you remember the story of the old man in Kafka's *The Trial?* He comes to the door of heaven and asks admittance. The keeper cannot grant him permission; so he waits before the open door for permission. He waits for days and years. Again and again he asks for permission, always to be denied. He grows very old and weak. He finally asks: "Why am I the only one seeking entrance at this door?" The doorkeeper replies: "This is your door. You did not enter, so now I am going to close it." Had the old man been less passive and more courageous, and had he walked by faith through that door, no one would have stopped him. Hope unaccompanied with faith to push ahead, is not hope at all, but blind resignation. Faith is the eyes of hope, "the substance of things hoped for" (Heb. 11:1).

Expectant hope keeps an open heart to victory. What is victory anyway? Is it to reach a certain goal? Is it to overcome something or someone? Is it simply to have your own way? Is it to achieve status in the eyes of the world? Is it to be crowned with laurels? Of course, all these are victories of a kind, but they are not Christian victory.

Christian victory is to win when you lose, to be well when you are sick, to walk straight when you are lame. It is even to live when you die. Christian victory is the acquisition of a certain kind of attitude and a very special power.

The final victory we hope for is also the victory of life over death. Strangely man spends a lot of time thinking about death, but not much time talking about it. If life is the enchantment of human dust, then death is its disenchantment.

Most people do not want to die and they spend their time

feverishly working to avoid death, yet they know that the fact of birth is an irrevocably commitment to death. They know they move mysteriously toward the end of life. They are caught in this inevitability just as they are caught in their sins. In fact, sin and death belong together, and it was for both that Christ came into the world to give us victory. Jesus put it simply: "I am the resurrection, and the life" (John 11:25). Paul said: "In Christ shall all be made alive. The last enemy that shall be destroyed is death . . . the sting of death is sin . . . . But thanks be to God, which gives us the victory through our Lord Jesus Christ" (1 Cor. 15:22,26,56,57).

Many years ago I had an experience which showed me how essential hope is to the sanity of man. It happened in a rural community where I was teaching school. The post oak leaves rattled like dry paper as the wind whipped them against the school house door. Even inside the children could feel the worst winter of their lives. They sat close to the stove which would devour a whole rick of wood before the let-out bell. Above the wind I heard a sound I had never heard before, the sobbing of a full-grown man. The children, busy with their lunch-time chatter, noticed nothing. Quickly I left the room and stood in the leaves. A man was leaning against the corner post and talking as though to the ground.

"I missed it. I missed the PWA truck. I will not get my day's work." He took a deep breath and cried out, "O Lord, what will I do?"

When he lifted his face, I saw two angry eyes, red with cold and grief. Ice was clinging to his moustache and his ragged scarf hid his chin. This was Mr. Moses whose son Joe had been out of school since Monday. That was the day the little boy had asked me for my apple core.

"What is wrong, Mr. Moses?"

"I missed the public works truck, and now I will not have money for medicine, much less food."

"What do you mean medicine?"

"Joe's got the measles. He can't breathe. Grannie says it's pneumonia and that he will die." He walked off through the sand toward home.

The wind had stopped and snow was falling when little Joe died with this father holding his hand. The county doctor who had come late in the day had done all he could. It was so quiet when I folded his bony arms across his chest that I could hear the rustling of the bright new quilt that covered him. His grannie had given it to him for his tenth birthday.

A few friends gathered the next day in the Brushy Church to comfort the family with their songs and prayers. As I read the twenty-third Psalm, the father uttered that same deep cry of sorrow that I had heard in the wind. "I've failed him. Oh, I failed my little boy," he said. Then I read: "Let not your heart be troubled: ye believe in God, believe also in me. In my father's house are many mansions, if it were not so, I would have told you. I go to prepare a place for you." (John 14:1–2). The father became very quiet. Someone took up the singing and the family came to tell the little boy good-by.

Mr. Moses looked at Joe, then at me and smiled. "It's true," he said. "It's true, it's true."

"What is true, Mr. Moses?"

"It's true that Joe is now where there is no cold, no hunger, no sorrow. He is in the house of many mansions."

Then something happened that I have never seen or heard at any other funeral. The grieved father lifted his voice in a quiet shout of praise to God. "Blessed be our God who gives us hope." He was still smiling when the last frozen clod was piled on the little mound.

The next day he brought me the quilt all washed and ironed. He said, "Joe knew he would not live. He wanted you to have this."

Many times I have looked at that quilt; I have remembered the love of a little boy and the hope of a father. I have remembered also the mysteries of life and death and the promise of

Christ: "I am the resurrection and the life: he that believeth in me, though he were dead, yet shall he live."

NOTES

1. Erich Fromm, *The Revolution of Hope* (New York: Harper and Row Publisher, 1968) p. 9.

2. *Ibid*, p. 14.

3. From *Still the Trumpet Sounds*, J. Wallace Hamilton. Copyright © 1970 by Fleming H. Revell Company, Old Tappan, New Jersey.

CHAPTER 10

Expectant Love

■ ■ ■

A mother once watched her child at play. Sticks and bottles became people with which he carried on conversations. Trees were given names and shadows were treated as things alive. Later she told his father: "Sometimes I think our little boy experiences a great loneliness." Another little boy sat under his mother's kitchen window and sang a song he had heard from an old phonograph record: "When I am gone, I will soon be forgotten." This mother too thought her son was experiencing loneliness.

Both mothers were probably only partly right. There is some loneliness in every child's life, yet there are other things often mistaken for loneliness, some of which are good and some bad. The little boy who made friends out of trees was experiencing solitude more than loneliness. His imagination and resourcefulness helped him turn what might have been restless loneliness into creative aloneness. I doubt that he was lonely because he knew what to do when he was by himself. The other child was not quite so creative, for very obviously in singing his sad song under his mother's window, he was making a bid for sympathy. He was not merely lonely, he was self-pitying. Solitude and self-pity are often mistaken for loneliness.

Depression is also mistaken for loneliness. A man finds the world becoming more unreal and his personal problems multiplying. Things around him slip out of focus and he loses his power for action. He is undergoing profound depression. Sometimes the cause of depression is physical such as metabolic disorders, deep low-grade infections, or other more serious diseases. It might come because of the sudden presence of more problems than can be solved. Job, for example, apparently underwent an overwhelming depression. The loss of property and family temporarily conquered him. Other times depression is caused by the upsetting of spiritual and psychological balance, as when one is seized with a profound pessimism or a deep sense of personal inadequacy. Depression, of course, can be accompanied with loneliness, but depression is not loneliness.

Loneliness has many definitions. It belongs to a family of words which includes alone, solitary, solitude, lonesome, and forlorn. Alone, solitary, and solitude are about the same. Alone stresses the objective fact of being entirely apart from others. Solitary denotes a personal sense of aloneness and solitude denotes an appreciation for aloneness. Alone and solitary apply to physical states of separation; solitude, to mental attitude. In loneliness, one feels alone and longs for companionship. Lonesomeness is heightened loneliness. Forlornness is heart-breaking loneliness; it sometimes marks the shift from loneliness to self-pity.

There are two kinds of loneliness, one which man makes for himself because of his sin. Man has a way of deliberately drawing the curtain between himself and others. In *The Minister's Black Veil,* Nathaniel Hawthorne tells of a minister who came to his pulpit one Sunday morning wearing a black veil. His congregation was appalled. When asked what it meant, he said that it was a symbol of sin and guilt. He wore the veil as long as he lived even though he admitted life was lonely and frightening behind the veil. People avoided him because of the veil, just as they avoided any person who draws the curtain between himself and them.

Dark terrible sin has a way of separating us from our loved ones. Liquor and drugs have broken up many a home. Uncontrollable temper or deep moodiness has erected walls between members of the same family. Unfaithfulness to a marriage vow has raised invisible barriers of suspicion and secretiveness between husbands and wives. Adam disobeyed God and ate the forbidden fruit. He became a divided person and from that time on lived at war with himself. Man is lonely because he is lost, and he is lost because he is a sinner.

Much of our loneliness arises from our indifference to people. If we dislike people, if we hurt people, if we move away from people, we must expect loneliness. We cannot go through life hurting others without driving them away from us. A very prominent man I know has a certain way of chilling the friendliness of others. He is often called "a cold fish." He seems so self-sufficient and many people think he is hateful because he feels strong. The truth is that he is hateful because he feels weak. He is caught in a box. Sin is on all sides of his lifelong indifference to people. The only way out is for him to turn around and accept people. He cannot do this, so in bitterness he lives a great loneliness, one of his own making.

People who do not make their loneliness but come into it because of their lots in life, have the best chance of doing something about it. A woman without children goes with her husband to the mental hospital and leaves him there for the rest of his life and goes home—this is loneliness. A man also without children stands strong while death takes his wife, his sisters, his brother, and he goes home—this is loneliness. A mother survives a terrible auto accident to be told that her husband and her children were all killed—this also is loneliness. Somehow or other, mostly with the help of God, people who suffer this kind of loneliness find ways of overcoming it better than those who make their own loneliness through sin and bad temper.

We are always tempted to think that loneliness is all bad, and that it is something from which we should escape as soon as possible. The truth is that loneliness has many good uses. For one thing, loneliness is the open door to a better understanding of ourselves and of life. Also, loneliness teaches a deeper appreciation for other people and their place in our lives. Perhaps the greatest thing loneliness does for us is to help us map the future. One young man I know never really faced the future of his life and started planning it in a sensible way until he experienced a long period of great loneliness.

The worst loneliness of all is that which man feels when he finally realizes that he is estranged from God. Even good men have at times a sense of this kind of loneliness. Our Savior prayed on the cross: "My God, My God, why hast thou forsaken me?" His was a voluntary estrangement that all men might be at peace with God. The moment of that cry was probably the loneliest moment in history, because he knew as no other has ever known, the true meaning of separation from God.

Men who have not consciously realized what separation from God means still suffer from it. Have you ever seen someone die suddenly from cancer? Well one day, deathly sick the next, they went to the grave so quickly. You say: "It was all so sudden." Yet when you think back you can see the marks of the disease in a change of attitude, loss of energy, the gradual weakening of the body, and in many other ways. They did not realize, you did not realize, but the disease was nevertheless present and doing its harm. So it is with man's estrangement from God. He suffers quite unaware from the greatest loneliness he has to bear, the loneliness of unforgiven sin that separates him from God.

It may sound strange to some, but there is a direct relationship of loneliness to love. Some people are lonely because they do not love and others are lonely because they do love. Love is the best escape from loneliness.

Some people are lonely because they do not love. Some of the most suffering persons are those hollow people who think only of themselves. They wallow in self-pity and fear. Not only do they live completely miserable lives themselves, they succeed in making other people miserable. There is only one love in this life, themselves; and everything they do turns around what is bad or good for them. They are totally absorbed in their own ego.

Self is a tremendously important thing, as Jesus plainly inferred when he said: "Love thy neighbour as thyself," but the self must somehow learn to transcend itself. The person whose spirit and attitude are always imprisoned inside himself, who has never realized that there are in the world other selves just as sensitive and just as important, and who fails to sense his own personality to the great diversity of life all about him, is destined to live a detestable lonely life. If one fails to transcend himself he experiences more and more withdrawal, which is a sign of the self turning back on itself and devouring itself.

Sometimes one lives selfishly to himself because from childhood he has been made too much aware of himself. A loving parent who wants his child to excel will set impossible goals and make the child self-conscious when he does not achieve them. Other parents will lavish too much praise on their child, complimenting him for achievements that are less than normal, and gradually building up in the child a wrong picture of himself. From earliest childhood, one like this has thought of himself as exceptional. He makes demands for special treatment and holds back himself as something special to be given only where the best is wanted and respected. People like this become prima donnas; they also are the friendless and the despised.

Another lives selfishly to himself because he has never been shown how to identify with a community of people. He cannot belong to a group. The old man who sets glumly in his darkened room, waiting for friends who never come, is likely to have been most of his life indifferent to groups. When young he found excuses not to visit the hospital or go to funerals. He ran from church groups and civic clubs. He spent much of his time alone simply because he did not know how to relate to groups of people. One with a lifetime habit of this kind of attitude is apt to get very bitter and very lonely in his old age.

Another lives selfishly alone because he is afraid. A man I

once knew owned a wholesale produce business. From the day he first opened his doors he was afraid he would fail. His life became one long nervous habit of distrust. He carried the only keys because he would not trust his employees. He moved his bank account to another town because he did not trust his banker. He worked from 5:00 A.M. to 7:00 P.M. because he was afraid if he did not work the business would bankrupt. He refused to go to church on Sunday, lest something should happen to his store. At about age fifty he suffered a cerebral stroke and spent the rest of his life in a rest home. Fear made him a completely selfish and detestable recluse. His habit of fearful thinking made him less and less lovable, and less and less able to love others. Even his wife had to quit seeing him at the rest home because he would turn on her with anger and hate. The strange thing about this man was that he had started life as tremendously well liked, having been voted the most popular boy in his high-school graduating class, but his fear tracked him down, isolated him, and destroyed him.

Loneliness has a way of feeding on itself and drawing those who allow it to dominate their lives into even greater dejection. A man who lives without proper love for his fellow human beings will create intolerant pressures on his own life. He cuts himself off from life-strengthening friendships. King Solomon, the wise writer of the Proverbs, said, "A man that hath friends must show himself friendly" (Prov. 18:24). It is as simple as this: Most people are not going to force their friendship on you. They will make a few simple gestures of friendliness, and will go out of the way to show you they care, but if you selfishly rebuff them, if you draw the curtain, they will quietly turn away to others more open to their love and appreciation. If you are in the habit of letting your friendships go because of your self-love, then be prepared for a lonely old age.

People who selfishly live to themselves are likely to become more and more bitter about life. The worst thing about selfishness is the anger it generates and the accusation it can bring.

Not long ago I saw a woman walking hand in hand with a woman that had just moved into our community. She was snatching at friendship wherever she could find it. In a glance I saw her whole life history. Selfish and bitter, she had driven her husband to divorce and alienated herself from her family. One by one she has made friends only to wreck them with her exaggerated loneliness and her bitter attacks on people who neglect her. She is one of those bitter people who pretend great independence but who constantly betrays her dependence. The most characteristic sign of her love of self is her insistence that her way is the only right way, and her ideas are the only true ideas. She once said to me: "No one knows how lonely I am." I wanted to add: "But everyone knows how selfish."

The unloving move slowly into the lonely world of unreality, which is another way of saying that they come nearer and nearer to insanity. People who selfishly cut themselves off from other people cut themselves off from the real world, and since everyone must have some kind of a world in which to live, they begin to put together a false world. They do not see the problems of life in perspective, and they invariably form wrong ideas of what it means to be at peace with their fellowmen. A young woman was deserted by her sweetheart within an hour of their marriage. She at once began to live a selfish life, retreating more and more to herself. She became very queer, and when she died alone, they found her trousseau stored in a coffin standing on end in her parlor. Her sister once said: "Her broken marriage did not destroy her; she destroyed it. Even as a child, she was the most selfish person I ever saw." Loneliness from lack of love is a morbid loneliness.

Some people are lonely because they do love. Loneliness that arises from love for others is a creative loneliness. It can be one of the great spiritual experiences of life. Once I went to look at a house for sale; the old man who owned it had decided time had come for him to move to a rest home. It was a very hot July day, and we talked for a while in the yard about the dry weather. Inside I was amazed to find the living room decorated for Christmas. There was a tree in the corner with the lights and tinsel snow, and over the doors bright-red bells and green garland. I remarked: "You are early with your decorations, my friend." His simple answer was: "No, those are last year's decorations. They are just like my wife put them up. It was one of the last things she ever did." There was nothing morbid or distasteful in what he said or the way he said it. As we talked I realized that here was a man experiencing deep lasting loneliness because of his love for one who could no longer be with him. He loved her so much that he left her Christmas things just the way she had placed them, yet he had decided time had come to move on, and he was about to find a new life in a rest home.

A mother whose children are scattered to the ends of the earth and who must spend long hours alone, is apt to be pensive about the busy years when her home was filled with laughter and tears of young people growing up. There is a scar on the wall where a tricycle banged against it, and behind a door there are marks and dates to show how fast her sons and daughters grew. She cannot bring herself to cover them. Even if she does cover them, she carries them in her heart and brings them out from time to time where she can see them. Hers is a loneliness born of great love. Her nostalgia is a good thing provided it does not cut off from the world or keep her from looking ahead.

The loneliness of great love is seen in the closing days of the life of Jesus on earth. In one of his last great sermons he said, "Greater love hath no man than this, that a man lay down his life for his friends" (John 15:13). Even when he said that one of his friends was plotting his death. A few hours later he went with three of his closest disciples to Gethsemane, and there leaving them he went a little farther to one of the loneliest places man has ever stood, to that moment when he must look death in the eye and say in prayer: "Father, if it be possible, let this cup pass from me: nevertheless not as I will, but as thou wilt" (Matt. 26:39). In that agonizing hour Jesus was tasting the loneliness of death for every man, for surely there is no hour so lonely as the one that comes when a man realizes that the rest of the world is going to live but he is going to die. Jesus suffered that moment of loneliness for you and me because of his deep love for us.

A little while later Judas met him at the brook called Kidron and betrayed him with a kiss, and here also Jesus tasted agonizing loneliness, the loneliness of betrayal by one whom you have chosen and loved. To be betrayed by people you don't know or don't like is tolerable, but to be betrayed by people you love is agonizing. Later that day when life was ebbing and he realized what a gulf there was between him and his enemies he prayed still another prayer of incomparable love and loneliness. "Father, forgive them; for they know not what they do" (Luke 23:34). Finally at the end he had a sense of being separated from him whom he loved the most and who loved him the most. He said: "My God, my God, why hast thou forsaken me?" (Matt. 27:46). Such loneliness the world has never seen before or since. That cry was the loneliness of all the love there was, transcending itself in death, and spending itself on behalf of the whole world. How much more lonely this lonely world would be if that lonely cry of love had never been uttered.

Love is the way to overcome great loneliness. Everyone must endure some loneliness. Even if we live with others, there are times when we must feel alone and unrelated. As we grow older, these moments of isolation come more often and linger longer, especially for people left alone in the world without family. Loneliness is surely a universal experience.

Many cures have been suggested for loneliness. Almost all of them point to cures outside of self, to some deed or action. The sound of them is very familiar. Go visit someone. Do a kind deed. Make a new friend. Join a social group. Get involved in community action. Identify with the church. Get a job.

All of these are very good provided deep down inside your spiritual attitude is right. At the bottom of everything must be love, not simply "I love you" love, but deep abiding appreciation for man's abiding humanity and for your own humanity. The real cure for loneliness is caught up in the words of Jesus: "Love thy neighbor as thyself." Creative identification with the world comes through love. We can love with the expectancy that it will work miracles, and we will not be disappointed.

Love will help us transcend ourselves. Man is lonely and forlorn, not because of his circumstances, but because of himself. As one small human being with limited experiences and a narrow range of life, if he lives totally within himself he is bound to reflect the smallness of his own private world. He will be like the man who takes his own pulse and listens to his own heartbeat. Nothing will sound right to him. He will exaggerate his own imperfections and create his own death. His need is to transcend himself, to get outside his own narrow world, to feel for others as he feels for himself. When Jesus asked us to love other people, he was prescribing not only what was best for them but what also is best for us. He knew that man does not really begin to live spiritually until he rises above himself and begins to take responsibility for people wherever he finds them.

Love helps us to establish empathy with others. The race in sorrow must have more than sympathy. It must have empathy, real spiritual identification with its heartbreak and suffering. The only way this is possible is through genuine love. Somehow there must come new understanding for people caught in the strange predicaments of life. Jesus said: "Be ye therefore merciful, as your Father also is merciful. Judge not, and ye shall not be judged: condemn not, and ye shall not be condemned: forgive and ye shall be forgiven. Give, and it shall be given unto you" (Luke 6:36–38).

Love helps break up self-pity. There are moments when everyone of us feels sorry for ourselves and will sigh deep sighs of self-pity, but unless we are careful, this can become a permanent state of mind for those of us who are lonely. Here again, love is the answer. Love opens our eyes to see that there are people whose lot in life is worse than ours, and whose lives can be blessed by some act of love.

Loneliness and love. The world is dying in loneliness for lack of love. In his famous play, *The Cherry Orchard,* Chekov portrays a decadent family quarreling with itself on the day the old homestead is sold for auction. The members desperately cling to each other, yet each of them is selfish and wilful. They hold together because of their common need for each other, but they fall apart because of terrible preoccupation with self. Every character is a study in great loneliness. As I read that play, I looked intensely into the background to see if I could discover any unifying force. There was none to be seen except the neglected cherry orchard. As the play closes, there rings across the stage the echoing sound of an ax as the trees are laid low by the new owner. The family fades to the four corners of the earth, and the old grandfather is left alone and forsaken. His words, the last to be heard, sum up the meaninglessness and the selfishness of life as they have lived it. He says: "They have gone . . . they have forgotten me . . . I'll lie down awhile . . . nothing's left, nothing . . ."

Pondering these words, one wonders, is this all there is to life? Is it true that many families who pretend to hold together really fall apart? Is the unity we see a hollow mockery? Is the real problem unutterable loneliness? Is real love lacking? Is the absence of love the reason for loneliness?

Yes. The answer is yes for a great many families, perhaps more than we would like to admit. The reason is that the family has not found an adequate unifying force outside itself. They do not have as much as a single cherished cherry tree to hold them together.

The head of Chekov's family was a middle-aged woman who had deserted her husband for a man with whom she kept house, but to whom she was not married. She loved him more than she loved her children. When she failed, all the others failed. Her infidelity casts a despairing gloom over everyone.

The thing really lacking in her life was a sense of the Eternal, the "Wholly Other" around which life let loose in this strange world must rally, else it perishes. Lacking God to mark her direction of responsibility, the needle in that mother's compass of life, fastened on one false god after another. No one in that family had any sense of spiritual direction. There was none to assauge their loneliness.

The thing missing in Chekov's family was genuine deep-down respect for the source and power of life, a sincere awe of the eternal, a sense of the love of God, an understanding of the love of Christ and the part it plays in making us ministers to each other's loneliness.

Worship died, and the family took its first steps to ruin. No family can truly survive with its members looking every different direction, and the only thing big enough and strong enough for them to see all at once is the love of God. The Bible warns the head of the family against spiritual destruction. "If any provide not for his own, and specially for those of his own house, he hath denied the faith, and is worse than an infidel" (1 Tim. 5:8). These are not threats but warnings.

True love has the power to set life in motion toward its own north star. It opens a man's mind to his own true nature. It liberates him from himself and gives him room to move. It helps him understand his limitations and learn how to escape from them. Love of God is every man's daily beginning point of success, for it is written: "Humble yourselves in the sight of the Lord, and he shall lift you up" (Jas. 4:10).